PASTA
COOKBOOK

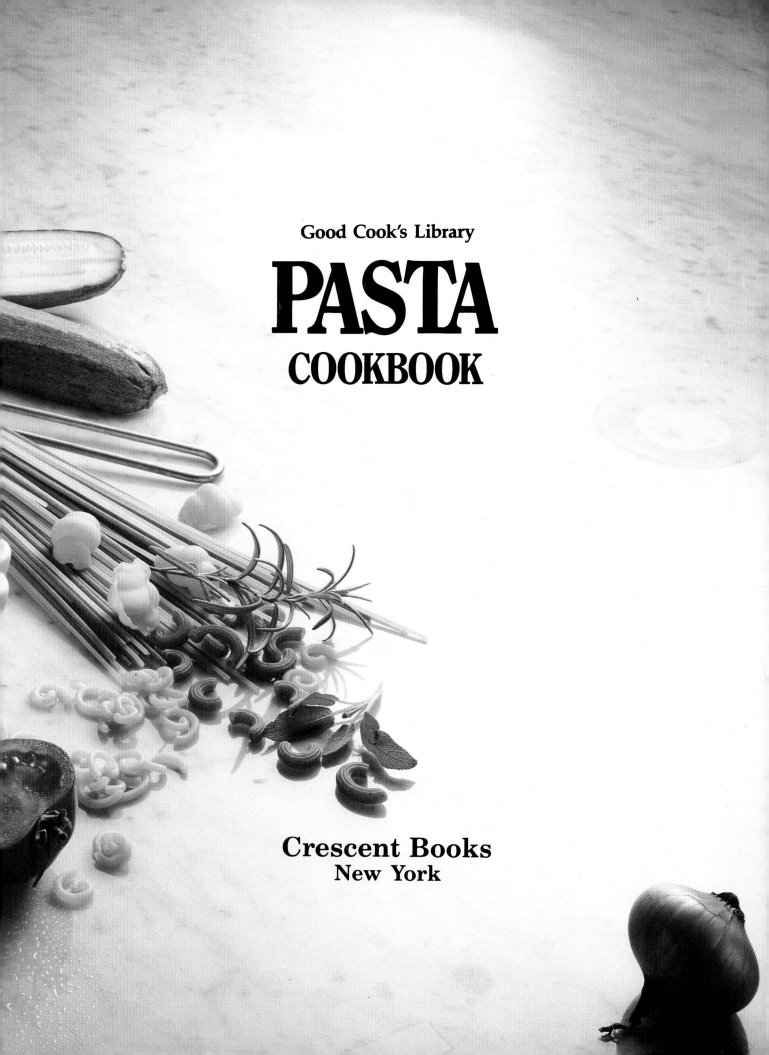

Good Cook's Library

PASTA
COOKBOOK

Crescent Books
New York

Contents

About this Book

This book is devoted exclusively to pasta, a subject close to the heart of many a gourmet. The diversity and almost unlimited creativity of pasta cookery, is shown in the brilliant color pictures, commissioned especially for trim basic.

Pasta is very adaptable and there are unlimited ways of serving it. Fine recipes appeal to the gourmet, hearty recipes are the favorites of families, and a party buffet without at least one pasta salad is incomplete. Pasta and enjoyment go together.

Start by flipping through this book and let yourself be tempted by the mouth-watering illustrations. The simply described recipes are easy to cook and instructions on preparation and cooking times will make it easy for you to plan appropriately.

The comments for each recipe indicate whether the dish is quick to prepare, time-consuming, economical or luxurious, or complicated. These comments also draw attention to classical recipes, national specialties or wholefood. Information about energy content—calories—and nutritional value—protein, fat and carbohydrates is included.

The book starts with what connoisseurs treasure most, home-made pasta. In this section step-by-step instructions show exactly how to make and shape pasta by hand. The use of a pasta-machine is also covered, as is the coloring of pasta dough with natural ingredients and the correct method of cooking pasta "al dente".

The first of the recipe sections is entitled "Pasta Soups and Starters." Alongside classical pasta soup with tomatoes you will find such recipes as Asian WonTon-Soup, Fettucine with Nuts and Sour Cream, or Spaghetti con aglio e olio (garlic and oil).

Enjoy browsing through "Pasta with Sauces and Ragouts." Spaghetti with Gorgonzola Sauce is prepared very easily. A somewhat more expensive but special dish for guests is Fettuccine with Pork Filet, or Pasta Twists with Rabbit Stew.

In the section on Pasta, Baked and Stuffed, you will most certainly find your old favorites. To these belong Lasagne al forno and traditional pasta and ham dishes. You can broaden your repertoire of recipes with a healthy wholemeal dish with fennel or an exclusive pasta soufflé with smoked salmon. In the foreign specialties, you will find Tyrolean Schlutzkrapfen and Russian pasta casserole and many others.

For summer evening meals, small get-togethers and party buffets, see the section on "Great Pasta Salads." Here you will learn how well pasta combines with many other ingredients. Cheese, tomatoes, poultry, meat, vegetables or fruit give these salads their varied and individual characters.

To round off the subject in "All about Pasta," the different types of pasta and their appropriate sauces are described. Cheese is almost always an accompaniment to pasta recipes, whether as a tasty main ingredient or spicy complement. To make the choice easy, the important types of cheese are described, and explain how to use which variety with which pasta recipe to best effect.

The team of authors have gathered together a wealth of recipes. Some of the team have personal connections with Italy and Austria, the Balkan countries, Spain, France, and Switzerland, as well as Japan, Korea or China, which are reflected in this book. Great pains have ben taken to fulfill the widest spectrum of choice for the simplest and the most fastidious reader, covering economical and luxurious recipes.

Wish you much enjoyment and fun cooking and eating these pasta dishes. Unless otherwise stated, all recipes are for 4 people.

The Value of Pasta

When one thinks about pasta, one thinks mainly of spaghetti, macaroni, pipes or ribbons, and perhaps even spätzle. The question of whether ravioli, gnocchi or even Chinese stuffed dumplings fall under the heading of "pasta" is answered positively when they can all be produced from a pasta dough, and can be dried and preserved. A great variety of pasta dishes are described throughout this book.

Some pasta is intended simply to be accompanied by a sauce; other pasta is destined for baking in the oven, to be stuffed, or as an ingredient in soups. Many pastas can be combined with ingredients you already have in the refrigerator, according to your taste and imagination. Pasta is simple to store; it will keep its flavor for over two years when stored in a cool dry place. Above all, beware of keeping pasta close to strongly-flavored foodstuffs, as it can pick up the odors of other foods, or experience some change in flavor.

Here's a tip for everyone with an interest in nutrition: pasta is by no means a foodstuff without nutritional value. If you are making use of industrially produced white-flour pasta, which only provides a few minerals, vitamins and fiber, you can raise the nutritional value of the meal by the accompaniments. Cheeses of all kinds, spicy sauces or vegetable mixtures are important components of pasta meals. Fresh salads or raw vegetables can be served with hot pasta dishes.

Almost all pasta is available in whole form. It is made of flour from whole grains, and contains a significant proportion of fiber. Wholemeal pasta is made from whole-wheat flour, rye flour, a mix-ture of both, or from wheat-meal. Anyone who is concerned about the higher nutritional value of wholemeal pasta and wishes to get accustomed to it, should begin

with the lighter kinds and gradually sample the completely dark rye pastas. If you've already discovered wholemeal pasta for yourself, the consumption of white flour pasta will reveal a lack of flavor. Wholemeal pastas do not become as sticky as white pasta if you happen to cook them for too long. They go best with well-flavored vegetable accompaniments and strong cheeses.

When buying industrially-produced wholemeal pasta, you will come across similar problems to those of wholemeal bread. For example, with some breads, a handful of whole grain in the dough qualifies the manufacturer to declare it "wholemeal." With caramel making it dark brown, it conveys the feeling of being "healthy" bread. As the situation is similar with wholegrain dough, the best guarantee of authentic nutritional value is to make your own wholemeal pasta. When making pasta, use only freshly milled wholegrain, since the nutritional value is quickly lost after milling and

can be conserved in baking or cooking. Only from freshly milled wholemeal flour can all the nutritional value be obtained, e.g. vitamin B complex, minerals and trace elements.

Whoever believes that pasta recipes comes only from Italy is mistaken. There are delicious and original Eastern pasta creations, which not only consist of tasty ingredients, but also provide dexterity in cooking. Eastern Europe, western Asia, the Near-East and the New World also have their own traditional pasta recipes. Whether Siberian pasta pouches, German stuffed pasta, spätzle, gnocchi or dumplings, each region has its own specialties.

The preparation of pasta is so uncomplicated and diverse in its variations, that it should be evident to ensure that these recipes always excel by using ingredients of the best quality. Here are some tips which can contribute to success in cooking pasta dishes.

- Always grate cheese just before using
- Only use fresh eggs (no more than 8 days old) in the preparation of pasta dough
- Use fresh herbs instead dried, and chop them just before needed in the recipe
- Don't use spices that have been stored for too long; grind or crush spices freshly before use.
- Use coconut butter, butter or goose-dripping to fry; for salads, use good quality olive oil that has not been stored for too long
- Season sparingly, preferably using herbs and other natural flavors, like yeast flakes, vegetable purées or garlic
- Make allowances for salty ingredients when seasoning
- Pay attention to the freshness of salads and vegetables
- Melted butter should be golden when drizzled over pasta, otherwise it will taste bitter
- With pasta recipes containing wine in the sauce, serve the same wine with the meal

Homemade Pasta

Making Noodle Dough

Making noodle dough yourself out of flour, eggs, some oil and salt is conceivably easy. It just takes a little time and you need to observe a few basic rules. For 4 people you will need 1 to 1⅓ cups of flour, 2 to 3 eggs, some salt and 2 to 3 teaspoons of oil. All the ingredients should be at the same temperature. The use of fresh country eggs results in a quality product that will satisfy the highest culinary expectations. Homemade noodle dough may be cut into flat noodles or other shapes, then loosely laid out on a floured kitchen towel and allowed to dry. Leave the noodles lying out until the are hard.

Sift the flour onto a wooden cutting board, make a well in the middle and pour in the eggs, oil and salt. Working from the inside to the outside, mix the ingredients together with your fingers. At the same time, use one hand to continually push the rim of flour up so that the eggs cannot run out.

Noodles Made by Machine

Kneading and rolling—which is basically all the work involved in making noodles—can be done by a simple, hand-operated machine. Various versions are available in specialty kitchen shops. Different attachments enable you to produce spaghetti or even to fill and cut out ravioli. Even though connoisseurs continue to praise noodles made entirely "by hand," the time saved by using a noodle machine is clearly an advantage. Dough made with the aid of such a machine does not require a resting period prior to further processing.

The dough ingredients are first kneaded by hand until the dough is no longer sticky. Open the machine as wide as possible and turn the lightly floured dough through the machine in smaller portions. Repeatedly gather up the dough and turn it through the machine again and again until it gleams and is as wide as the roller.

Coloring Noodles

Making flavored noodles in natural colors requires a little more time and effort than plain noodles. The visual and tasty versions certainly are worth the extra effort. Finely chopped or pureed, blanched spinach provides a deep, green color. Mixed chopped herbs result in a speckled green appearance. Mix in a pinch of saffron or tomato puree and you get variously colored orange noodles. Pureed red beets make the noodles dark red. Since most coloring ingredients contain quite a lot of liquid, it is necessary to add extra flour while you are kneading. When the dough is rolled out, the working surface also requires continual reflouring.

Blanch the spinach, rinse it quickly under cold water, drain and press it out very well. Puree and combine with flour, eggs, oil and salt. If the dough is going to be kneaded and rolled by a noodle machine, finely chopped spinach may be used.

Correctly Cooking Noodles

One of the basic rules when preparing noodle dishes: The pasta must never be overcooked. Repeated taste tests are necessary to gauge the correct consistency. The noodles should neither be hard nor may they taste like flour. Instead, there must still be a slight resistance to the bite and, at the same time, they must be elastic. Then they are "al dente," that is chewy, yet tender. Noodles taste best when they have just been cooked. They must first be drained; then they may be served with a vegetable or meat sauce and, if desired, sprinkled with freshly grated cheese.

For 1 pound of noodles, bring 4 quarts of water to a boil. Add 2 teaspoons of salt. 1 tablespoon of oil in the water keeps the noodles from sticking to each other or to the bottom of the pot while they are cooking. Slowly slide the spaghetti over the rim of the pan into the rapidly boiling water.

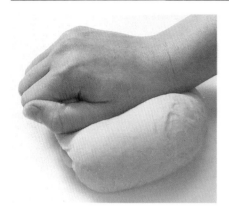

Knead the clump of dough: Repeatedly flatten it with the palms of your hands, fold together and flatten again until you obtain a gleaming and supple ball. This will take 10 to 15 minutes. If the dough becomes too stiff, work some additional water into it. Allow the dough to rest for 1 hour under an inverted bowl.

On a floured working surface, roll out the dough as thinly as possible; for filled noodles roll out to a thickness of $1/8$ to $1/10$ inch. Using a dough cutter cut into any desired shape. Or roll up the dough and cut out flat noodles using a sharp knife. Allow unfilled noodles to dry briefly before cooking.

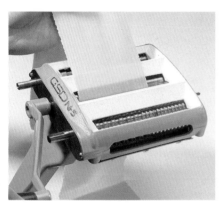

When you are ready to roll out the dough, decrease the width of the roller until you obtain the desired dough thickness. Discontinue folding the dough, so that it now becomes longer and thinner. When you are turning it through, make sure that the dough does not fold up on top of itself. Instead let it glide out onto the working surface like a ribbon.

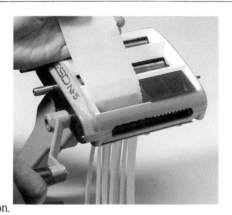

Change the machine's attachments. Using the cutting roller, cut the dough to the desired width. Allow the flat noodles, tagliatelle or spaghetti to dry for about 30 minutes before you cook them by laying them on a floured kitchen towel or, if they are quite long, over the arm of a chair.

For making orange or light red noodles, add to the noodle ingredients either thick, cooled tomato puree that has been spiced with finely chopped herbs, a few tablespoons of canned tomato paste or $1/8$ teaspoon of saffron. Knead the dough and roll it out.

Depending on their size, cook unpeeled red beets for 40 minutes to $1\frac{1}{2}$ hours until tender. Then peel, chop and puree them. Combine with the usual ingredients and knead into a noodle dough. The red beets must be completely cooled before they are combined with the dough ingredients.

Stir the noodles once with a wooden spoon. Make a taste test to determine doneness a few minutes before the cooking time indicated on the package is finished. Homemade noodles need only about half the amount of time.

Pour the noodles into a sieve. If they are going to be used for casseroles or salads, they should quickly be rinsed with cold water. If you are using "pasta asciutta" (dry noodles), then simply drain them and immediately mix with the sauce. If you need to set them aside for a few minutes, place them in a warm oven.

Homemade Pasta

Homemade Tortellini

Today, you can buy freshly made tortellini in almost any well-stocked supermarket or delicatessen. But the taste of homemade tortellini filled with delicious pureed or finely chopped farces maded of shrimp, cheese and spinach mixtures or meat can hardly be beat. You may arbitrarily vary the ratio of ingredients in a filling or you may add additional kinds of vegetable and use any kind of meat desired (the meat must however be precooked). And, preparing tortellini is not at all as difficult as generally assumed.

Roll the dough out to ⅛-inch thickness. Cut out rounds measuring 1½ inches in diameter. Cover any dough that is not immediately being worked with a damp cloth. With a teaspoon, drop the prepared filling made of seasoned tartare (ground sirloin), chopped onion, chopped salami, 1 egg yolk and grated cheese onto the rounds.

Constructing Lasagne

You don't really have to be an expert chef to attempt making an authentic lasagne, however you should be a great cooking buff since preparing all the necessary ingredients requires lots of time. Lasagne noodles are easy to make yourself; but if you want to skip this step, you can buy dried ones. Italian "sugo," the typical meat-based Italian sauce, requires a long period of simmering before it is thick and creamy. Then the Bechamel sauce must still be prepared in advance. And, finally, parmesan cheese must be freshly grated. Now you are ready to begin layering the lasagne.

Thoroughly grease a flat, rectangular casserole pan with butter. Cover the bottom of the pan with the meat sauce. Coat it with a layer of Bechamel sauce. Lay just cooked, homemade lasagne noodles on top. Dried lasagne noodles that require no precooking are also available commercially.

Sauce Bolognese

This is the sauce needed for lasagne. It's the spicy "sugo" from Bologna and it tastes delicious with spaghetti too. It's worthwhile making large quantities in advance, because it freezes well and can always function as the basis of a fine meal. The version described here, which requires a bit more work, is considered to be the original recipe.

Cook ¼ pound bacon in 2 tablespoons olive oil over very slow heat. Stir in and saute one each of the following diced vegetables: onion, carrot, celery stalk and clove of garlic. Add 1 pound ground meat (beef and/or pork) and continue to saute until the meat becomes grey.

Pesto

Pesto is a sauce that requires no cooking. There are various methods for producing "pesto," a green paste made with basil leaves. The basic ingredients always combine basil, garlic, pine nuts, cold-pressed olive oil and a freshly grated, piquant cheese like parmesan or pecorino. Pesto tastes delicious with all kinds of freshly cooked, preferably homemade noodles. In Genoa it is stirred into the minestrone by the spoonful. Whenever fresh basil is available, it is advisable to make larger quantities of pesto and freeze it in smaller portions. It's a very pleasant surprise on a cold winter's day!

Using a mortar and pestle, pulverize 2 diced cloves of garlic with 1 heaping tablespoon pine nuts. Then add basil leaves that have been washed and blotted dry. Grind them as well.

Brush the rims with water. Fold the rounds in half and press firmly. Carefully wrap the crescents around your index finger into the shape of a ring and press the ends together.

Cook the tortellini in rapidly boiling water for 8 to 10 minutes. Drain and serve sprinkled with melted butter and browned bread crumbs. A sauce that augments the filling may be offered with the tortellini.

Place a second layer of meat sauce and Bechamel sauce on top. Cover it with a final layer of noodles. Brush with Bechamel sauce making sure that no corners of the noodles are left exposed since they will quickly dry out during baking.

Finally, generously sprinkle the lasagne with freshly grated parmesan cheese, which may be mixed with bread crumbs if desired. Tiny cubes of mozarella or flakes of butter may also be sprinkled on top.

Pour in ½ cup red wine, leave the pan uncovered and allow the liquid to steam off. Then add 1 cup boiling beef bouillion and 1 pound peeled and finely diced tomatoes. Allow the liquid to steam off again. Crush the tomatoes with a wooden spoon.

Season the sauce bolognese with freshly chopped parsley, dried oregano, tomato paste, salt and pepper. Partially cover and simmer over low heat for 1 hour. Occasionally stir the sauce.

Transfer the mixture to a bowl and, while stirring constantly, alternately add 1 tablespoon grated cheese and a few drops of olive oil. An electric hand mixer or kitchen machine can be quite helpful here.

In this way, mix in all the grated cheese (¼ cup each of parmesan and pecorino) and about 5 tablespoons olive oil. Season the pesto with salt and freshly grated black pepper, cover and allow to rest for at least 1 hour. Before serving, mix in 2 tablespoons of the hot noodle water.

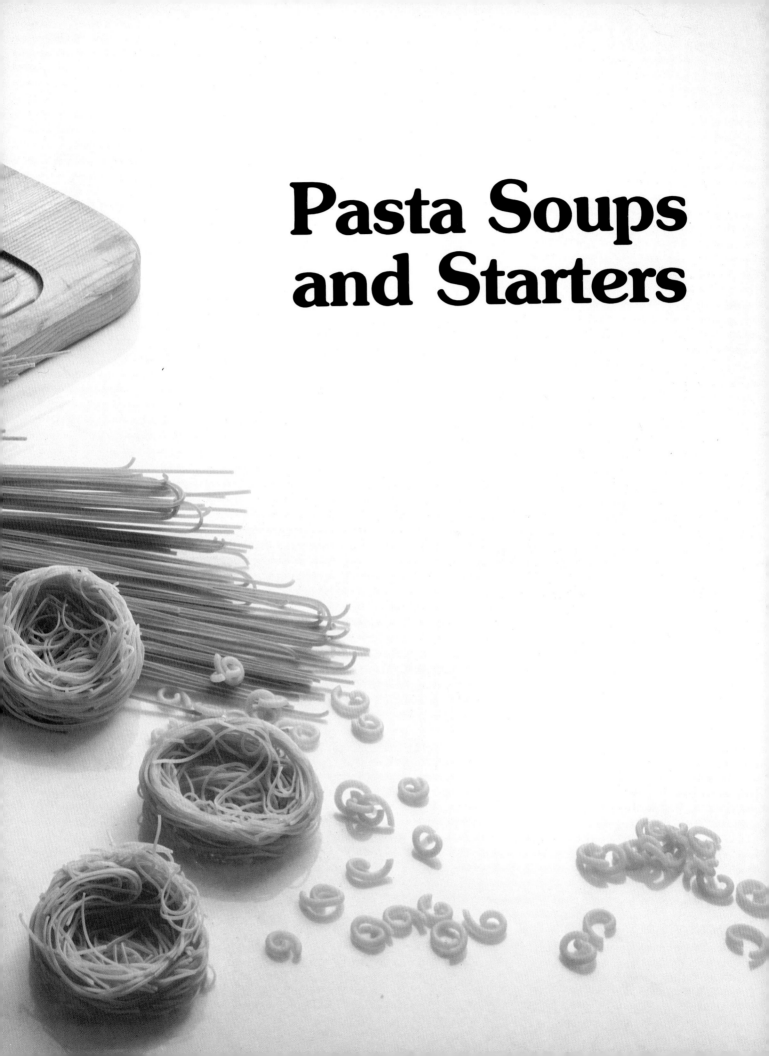

Pasta Soups
and Starters

Herb Soup with Pasta

Quick, economical

200 calories per person
Cooking time: 30 minutes

½ head lettuce
½ bunch each of chives, dill and parsley
2 sprigs basil
4 cups chicken bouillon
½ cup vermicelli (capellini)
½ cup shelled peas
1 tsp. butter
1 pinch each of salt and freshly milled white pepper
1 pinch of freshly grated nutmeg
4 egg yolks

Tear the lettuce into leaves, dry and cut into strips. Wash the herbs and pat dry. Chop the chives, dill and parsley finely, and pluck the small leaves off the basil. Bring the chicken bouillon to a boil, and add the pasta and peas. Let the soup cook, partially covered, on a moderate heat for 4 minutes. Place the finely chopped herbs, the lettuce strips and the butter in the soup, and heat briefly. Season the soup with salt, pepper and nutmeg. Gently slide 1 egg yolk into each soup-plate or cup, pour the soup over, and sprinkle basil over. Serve at once.

Austrian Specialty

Easy, economical

170 calories per serving
Drying time: 1 day
Preparation time: 40 minutes
Cooking time: 5 minutes

For the dough:
1 cup flour
1 pinch of salt
1 egg
For the soup:
1 tbs. sunflower oil
4 cups hot vegetable broth
1 tbs. dried mushrooms
1 pinch each salt and freshly grated nutmeg
1 egg yolk
½ bunch parsley

Sift the flour on to a board, make a hollow in the middle, add the egg and salt, and knead to a firm, smooth dough; gradually add a little more flour. Rub the dough through a medium-sized grater, and spread the "pearls" out to dry on a cloth overnight. • Heat the oil in a saucepan. Brown the "pasta pearls" until golden, stirring. Pour the vegetable broth over and bring to a boil. Wash the dried mushrooms thoroughly in a sieve, and add them to the soup. Cook it all for 5 minutes. • Season the soup with nutmeg and salt, and remove from the heat. Blend the egg yolk with 1 tbs. of hot soup, and thicken the soup with it. • Wash the parsley, pat dry, chop finely and sprinkle over the soup.

Tip: The dough needs to be firm for grating. It is a good idea to place the roll of dough in the freezer for 15 minutes before grating. Well-dried "pasta pearls" can be stored in a tightly sealed jar for up to one month.

Fettucini and Chickpea Soup

Economical but lengthy cooking time

310 calories per serving
Preparation time: 12 hours (including soaking peas)
Cooking time: 1 hour 40 minutes

2 cups chickpeas
½ tsp. of salt
2 sprigs rosemary
3 garlic cloves
3 oz. lean bacon
4 cups (approx.) clear beef bouillon
¾ cup fettucini
Pinch each of salt and fresh ground white pepper
4 tbs. grated Parmesan cheese

Cover the chickpeas with lukewarm water and leave to soak for 12 hours. • Drain, cover with fresh salted water and bring to a boil. • Wash the rosemary. Peel the garlic cloves. Simmer the chickpeas covered, with 1 garlic clove and 1 sprig of rosemary over a moderate heat for about 1½ hours. • Chop the bacon, the leaves from the remaining sprig of rosemary and the garlic very fine. • Strain the cooked chickpeas, retaining the cooking liquid. Cover the chickpeas and keep warm. Discard the rosemary sprig and garlic cloves. • Add the cooking liquid to the beef bouillon to make up to 6 cups, and bring to a boil once. Stir the chopped rosemary, garlic cloves and bacon into the soup, add the fettucini until just cooked, but not too soft. • Season the soup with salt and pepper and reheat the chickpeas in the soup; do not allow the soup to come to a boil again. Serve with grated Parmesan.

Pasta Soup with Basil

Easy, economical

290 calories per serving
Preparation time: 15 minutes

1½ cups potatoes, cooked until floury
6 cups vegetable bouillon
2 ripe beefsteak tomatoes
¾ cup spaghetti
1 bunch basil
½ tbs. cold-pressed olive oil (virgin oil)
Pinch each of salt and freshly ground white pepper
2 tbs. of freshly grated Parmesan cheese

Wash and peel the potatoes, rinse again, cut into small dice, and simmer in the vegetable broth for approx. 25 minutes. • Cut the tomatoes crosswise, plunge into boiling water, remove skins, and add to the diced potato after 15 minutes cooking time. • Break the spaghetti into pieces, place in the soup until just cooked but not too soft— about 5 minutes. • Wash the basil and pat dry. Strip the leaves from the stem and chop. • Stir the oil into the soup, and season. • Serve the soup in 4 soup plates, each garnished with basil and ½ tbs. Parmesan cheese.

Sauerkraut Soup

Complete meal recipe

900 calories per serving
Preparation time: 30 minutes

2 onions
2 tbs. sunflower oil
½ tbs. buckwheat
1 tbs. coarse ryemeal
2¼ cups sauerkraut
1 bouquet garni
5 cups water
1 bay leaf
Small horn-shaped pasta
4 spicy sausages
1 tbs. freshly chopped parsley
1 tsp. vegetable bouillon powder
1–2 pinches freshly ground black pepper
½ tsp. paprika

Peel and chop the onions finely. • Heat the oil in a large pan, and sauté the onion. Add the buckwheat and the ryemeal and cook together, stirring for 1 minute. Chop the sauerkraut, and add it to the vegetable/grain mixture. Add the bouquet garni and bay leaf. Cover and cook over low heat for 15 minutes. • Bring the salted water to a boil, and cook the pasta for about 10 minutes, drain in a sieve and add to the soup. • Cut the sausages into slices and mix into the soup. Discard the bay leaf. Stir in the parsley, and season the soup with the vegetable bouillon powder, pepper and paprika.

Peasant Soup

Complete meal recipe

290 calories per serving
Preparation time: 15 minutes
Cooking time: 10 minutes

5 cups water
About ½ tbs. vegetable bouillon powder
1 bouquet garni
½ cup buckwheat
1¼ cups potatoes
1¼ cups shelled green peas
¾ cup green wholewheat pasta
½ bunch dill
1 tbs. cream
½ tbs. butter
1 pinch freshly ground white pepper

Bring the water, the bouillon powder, the bouquet garni and the buckwheat to a boil. Meanwhile, peel, wash, and dice the potatoes, and add them to a boiling stock with the peas and pasta. Cook together 10 minutes. • Wash the dill, pat dry and chop the leaves finely, discarding the stem. Remove the pan from heat. Mix cream, butter and chopped dill into the soup and season to taste with pepper and a little more vegetable bouillon powder.

Tip: If required, the soup may be made even more substantial by scattering 1 cup of crisply grilled, chopped bacon over the portions. Chervil may be substituted for dill. With fresh fruit for dessert, this makes a "quick" menu.

Genoese Vegetable Soup

Italian specialty

310 calories per serving
Preparation time: 80 minutes

2 medium onions	
1 cup zucchini	
½ cup carrots	
¾ cup string beans	
2 tbs. olive oil	
6 cups hot vegetable broth	
1 pinch each salt and freshly ground black pepper	
3 garlic cloves	
1 cup rosmarini (rice shaped pasta)	
½ bunch each basil and parsley	
1 tbs. freshly grated Pecorino cheese (ewes-milk cheese)	

Peel the onions and chop finely. Wash and top and tail the zucchini. Scrape the carrots under running water and dice. Also dice the zucchini. Wash and drain the beans, and break into small pieces. • Heat the olive oil in a saucepan. Fry the chopped onions until transparent, add the diced vegetables and beans and fry for 10 minutes, stirring often. • Pour the vegetable broth over, cook the soup for 15 minutes, and season to taste. • Peel the garlic cloves, chop very finely, and cook with the soup for a short while. • Add the pasta and cook for a few minutes until 'al dente'. • Wash the herbs, pat dry, and strip off the leaves from the stems before chopping the leaves. Serve the soup, garnished with herbs and cheese.

Pasta Soup with Savoy Cabbage

Economical, easy

250 calories per serving
Preparation time: 1 hour

½ savoy cabbage, approx. 1¼ lbs.	
1 onion	
½ tbs. olive oil	
Pinch of freshly grated nutmeg	
6 cups hot beef broth	
¾ cup pasta shells	
1 bunch parsley	
Pinch each of salt and freshly ground black pepper	
1 tbs. freshly grated Pecorino (ewes-milk) cheese or Parmesan cheese	

Discard the outer leaves from the savoy cabbage, cut through the half, and discard the hard stalk. Shred the quarters of cabbage finely, rinse in a sieve and drain well. Peel the onion and cut into thin rings. • Heat the oil, and fry the onion rings until transparent. Add the shredded cabbage and cook approx. 10 minutes, stirring occasionally. • Season the cabbage with the nutmeg, and pour the beef broth over. Cook the cabbage in a covered pan over low heat for 30 minutes. • Cook the pasta shells in the soup until 'al dente'. • Wash the parsley, pat dry, discard the stems and chop the leaves finely. • Season the soup with salt and pepper to taste, and serve with grated cheese and parsley.

Beef and Bean Soup with Pasta

Takes time

400 calories per serving
Preparation time: 2½ hours
Ingredients for 8 servings

2½ qts. water
1 tsp. salt
2¼ lbs. beef (ribs)
Some bones for soup
1 onion
1 bouquet garni
2¼ cups string beans
1 cup vermicelli (capellini)
1 clove garlic
½ bunch each chives and parsley
Pinch black pepper

Bring the salted water to a boil. Wash the meat and bones. Peel the onion and add it with the bouquet garni, meat and bones to boiling water. Simmer the meat gently for 2 hours; during the first 15 minutes remove the scum from the surface. • Clean the beans, wash, cut into pieces and cook covered in salted water for 15 minutes. Cook the pasta in salted water for about 4 minutes, drain and leave to cool in colander. • Peel the garlic and chop finely. • Remove the bones from the stock, and carefully discard the fat and sinews, dicing the remaining meat carefully. Strain the stock. • Wash the herbs, pat dry and chop finely. Add the beans, the diced meat, the garlic and the vermicelli to the stock. Season and sprinkle with herbs.

Neapolitan Pasta Soup

Italian specialty

230 calories per serving
Soaking time: 12 hours
Preparation time: 20 minutes
Cooking time: about 1 hour

½ cup butterbeans
4 cups water
1 bouquet garni
4 tsp. powdered vegetable bouillon
½ cup wholewheat noodles
1 tsp. salt
2¼ cups tomatoes
1 clove garlic
6 tbs. olive oil
2 tsp. freshly chopped or ½ tsp. dried oregano
Pinch cayenne pepper

Leave the beans to soak in 4 cups water overnight. • Drain the beans through a colander and place in 4 cups fresh water with the bouquet garni and 2 teaspoons instant bouillon powder to simmer for about 45 minutes in a covered pan. • Cook the noodles in fast boiling salted water for about 7 minutes until 'al dente', then strain, rinse in cold water and set aside. Dip the tomatoes briefly into boiling water, peel, discard the stalky part, and dice the flesh. • Peel and finely chop the garlic, and fry in the oil until transparent. Add the diced tomato, oregano and cayenne pepper, and cook the tomato sauce, stirring, for 5 minutes, then mix with the noodles into the bean soup. • Reheat the soup briefly, and season with the remaining vegetable bouillon powder.

Tomato Soup with Ricotta Gnocchi

A meal in itself, economical

260 calories per serving
Preparation time: 40 minutes

2 ripe beefsteak tomatoes	
2 tbs. butter	
1 tsp. wholemeal flour	
4 cups hot vegetable broth	
Pinch each salt and freshly milled white pepper	
2 sprigs thyme	
1 sprig rosemary	
2 hardboiled eggs	
¼ cup butter	
1 egg	
2 tbs. ricotta cheese	
3 tbs. wholemeal flour	
Pinch each salt and freshly grated nutmeg	

Make a cross in the skin of the bottom of the tomatoes with the point of a knife, and immerse the tomatoes briefly in boiling water. Remove skin and stalky part in middle. Chop the flesh. • Melt the butter, and fry the flour until golden. Stir in the chopped tomatoes, and pour in the vegetable broth. Season with salt, pepper, leaves of thyme and rosemary, and cook for 10 minutes. • To make the dumplings, shell the hardboiled eggs, chop, and mash with a fork, add the butter, the egg, the ricotta and the flour to a smooth, pliable but firm dough. Season with salt and nutmeg. • Dip a teaspoon in hot water and use to shape the dumplings. Let the ricotta dumplings cook in the soup, until they rise to the surface; the soup should only be simmering gently.

Pea Soup with Flour Gnocchi

Easy, economical

330 calories per serving
Preparation time: 15 minutes
Cooking time: 20 minutes

1 small bundle leeks	
½ cup carrots	
1 tbs. cooking oil	
1 cup shelled green peas	
4 cups hot chicken broth	
1 egg	
¼ cup soft butter	
¾ cup flour	
½ tsp. dried mixed herbs	
Pinch salt and mild paprika	
10 small leaves peppermint	

Remove the dark green tops of leaves and the root ends from the leeks. Cut in half lengthwise, wash thoroughly and cut into julienne strips. Scrape and wash the carrots, cut lengthwise and then cut into small strips. • Heat the oil in a saucepan and stir fry the vegetable strips with the peas, add the chicken broth, and cook for 15 minutes. • To make the gnocchi, mix the egg and butter well with a fork. Add the flour and dried herbs, and knead to a pliable dough. • Dip a teaspoon into a boiling soup and use it to shape the gnocchi. Let the gnocchi cook in the soup until they rise to the surface. Season the pea soup with salt and paprika. • Wash the mint leaves, chop finely and use to garnish.

Jewish Kreplach (Shell Shapes)

Takes time

330 calories per serving
Preparation time: 40 minutes
Resting time: 1 hour
Cooking time: 10 minutes

2 eggs
½ tsp. salt
1 tbs. oil
¾–1 cup flour
1 cup cooked chicken
2 tbs. chopped parsley
1 small onion
1 tbs. goose-dripping
½ tsp. salt
Pinch each black pepper and ginger powder
4 cups chicken broth (home-made or instant)

Mix the eggs with the salt and oil. Gradually add the sifted flour, to make a firm dough. • Mince the chicken meat as finely as possible, and add 1 tablespoon parsley to it. Peel the onion, chop finely and add to the meat with the dripping, salt, pepper and the ginger. • Roll out the dough to ⅟₁₆ in. thick and cut into squares of approx. 2 in. Divide the stuffing between the squares. Fold each square in half diagonally, and use a fork to crimp the edges together firmly. Leave the stuffed pasta shapes to dry on a floured cloth for 1 hour. • Bring the chicken broth to a boil, and gently cook the pasta shapes for 10 minutes. • Serve the soup garnished with the re-maining parsley.

Siberian Pasta Shapes

Takes time

450 calories per serving
Preparation time: 45 minutes
Resting time: 1 hour
Cooking time: 10–15 minutes

2½ cups flour
2 eggs
½ tsp. salt
1 small onion
½ lb. ground beef
½ tsp. salt
Pinch freshly milled white pepper
1 egg yolk
4 cups beef broth (home-made or instant)
½ bunch dill

Knead the flour with the eggs, salt and as much lukewarm water as necessary to make a firm but pliable pasta dough. • Peel the onions, chop very finely and mix into the ground beef with the salt and pepper. • Roll the dough out to ⅟₁₆ in. thickness on a lightly floured surface and cut out cir-cles of about 1½ in. in diameter. Paint the edges with lightly beaten yolk of egg. • Divide the ground meat stuffing between the pieces of dough, fold each piece in half and press the edges together with a fork. Leave stuffed pasta shapes to rest for 1 hour. • Bring the beef broth to a boil, and simmer the pasta shapes for about 10–15 minutes. • Wash and chop the dill and use to garnish the soup before serving.

Pasta Soup with Tomatoes

Simple

200 calories per serving
Preparation time: 40 minutes

4 large ripe tomatoes
4 cups water
2 vegetable bouillon cubes
1 tsp. oil
½ cup vermicelli (capellini)
3 eggs
2 tsp. lemon juice
2 tbs. freshly chopped herbs, e.g. chives, basil or parsley

Make a cross in the skin at the bottom of each tomato with a sharp knife, cover with boiling water, and leave for a few minutes. • Bring the water to a boil and dissolve the bouillon cubes. • Remove the tomato skins, chop the flesh into chunks and discard the stalky center. Sieve or liquidize the tomato flesh, and add to the stock with the oil. Bring the soup back to a boil. Drop in the vermicelli and cook until 'al dente'—about 4 minutes. • Take the soup off the heat and keep warm, covered. • Separate the eggs. Beat egg whites with lemon juice until stiff. Blend in the yolks one at a time into the whites, with an egg-whisk. • Gradually stir 8 table-spoons of hot soup into the egg mixture. Then blend the egg mixture into the remaining soup. • Garnish the tomato soup with herbs.

Winter Vegetable Soup with Pasta

Takes time

220 calories per serving
Preparation time: 30 minutes
Cooking time: 25 minutes

1 small rutabaga (1¾ cup)
¼ celery (1 cup)
2 carrots (1 cup)
¼ white cabbage
1 large onion
1 tbs. oil
4 cups hot beef broth (instant)
½ cup vermicelli (capellini)
1 tbs. freshly chopped parsley

Wash the rutabaga, celery and carrots under running cold water, peel or scrape, rinse again and slice thickly. Remove the outside leaves from the white cabbage, cut out and discard the center core, wash and shred. Peel and chop the onion. • Heat the oil in a sufficiently large pan, and fry the onions until trans-parent, stirring constantly. Add the remaining vegetables, briefly turning them in the oil and pour over the beef broth. Cook the vegetables, covered, for about 20 minutes. • Add the vermicelli, stir the soup thoroughly and cook for about 4 minutes, until the pasta is 'al dente'. Serve gar-nished with chopped parsley.

Tip: The soup tastes even better when served with 1 tablespoon of sour cream to each portion.

Pasta Soup with Borlotti Beans

Takes time, economical

450 calories per serving
Soaking time: 12 hours
Preparation time: 15 minutes

1 cup dried borlotti beans
1 small onion
2 cloves garlic
⅓ cup lean bacon
1 cup ripe tomatoes
1 bunch parsley
4 tbs. olive oil
4 cups beef broth, approx.
1 tsp. mixed dried herbs
Pinch of black pepper
¾ cup ditali
2 tbs. freshly grated Parmesan cheese

Soak the beans in water overnight. • Cook the beans in the soaking water for approx. 1 hour until soft, then drain in colander. Meanwhile, peel the onion and garlic and chop finely. Dice the bacon, peel the tomatoes and cut into pieces. Wash and pat dry the parsley, and chop finely. • Heat the oil in a sufficiently large saucepan, and cook the onion and garlic until transparent. Add the bacon, parsley, tomatoes and beans, and simmer, covered, for about 20 minutes. Sieve or liquidize half of the mixture. Pour the bean cooking liquid on to the unsieved vegetables and add beef broth, to bring to 6 cups. • Continue cooking the soup: season with mixed dried herbs and pepper. Cook the ditali in the soup until 'al dente' and whisk the vegetable purée into the soup. Heat the soup thoroughly and sprinkle with grated cheese before serving.

Potato and Pasta Soup

Economical, easy

430 calories per serving
Preparation time: 45 minutes

1 medium sized onion
¼ lb. lean bacon
1¼ cup waxy potatoes
2 tbs. butter
6 cups beef broth
Pinch each salt and freshly milled white pepper
1 cup spaghetti hoops
2 tbs. freshly chopped parsley

Peel the onions and cut into small dice. Likewise, dice the bacon. Wash, peel and rinse the potatoes, and cut into paper thin slices. • Heat the butter in a saucepan and fry the bacon and onions, stirring constantly for 10 minutes until golden. • Pour the beef broth over, and season with salt and pepper. Bring to a boil and add the sliced potatoes; cook for 10 minutes. Add the spaghetti hoops to the pan, stir well and leave on the heat uncovered until the pasta is just cooked, but not too soft. Sprinkle the parsley over the soup before serving.

Tip: 1 or 2 cloves garlic can be substituted for the onion, and to save calories, 1 cup mushrooms for the bacon.

Zucchini & Pasta Soup

Simple, economical

290 calories per serving
Preparation time: 1 hour

1 onion
2¼ cups smallest zucchinis
2 ripe beefsteak tomatoes
4 tbs. olive oil
6 cups hot beef broth
¾ cup spaghetti hoops
½ bunch each of basil and parsley
Pinch each salt and freshly milled white pepper
2 tbs. grated Pecorino (ewes-milk cheese) or Parmesan

Peel and chop the onions finely. Wash, dry, and top and tail and dice the zucchini. Cut the tomatoes across, blanch in boiling water, peel, cut into pieces and discard the stalky center. • Heat the oil in a large pan. Fry the onion until transparent, add the diced zucchini and pieces of tomato and saute, stirring constantly. Pour the beef broth over and bring to a boil. Add the pasta, stir once and cook 6 minutes until 'al dente'. Wash and pat dry the herbs, and chop the leaves finely. Stir into the soup and season with pepper. Before serving add grated cheese.

Soup with Home-made Pasta

A meal in itself

310 calories per serving
Preparation time: 15 minutes

¼ cup each fine millet-flour and soya flour
1 tsp. mixed dried herbs
½ tsp. Delikata (flavoring spice from health food shop)
½ tsp. Kurkuma powder
1 small egg
1 tbs. sesame seed oil
1¼ cup new potatoes
¾ cup carrots
¼ cup butter
1¼ cups shelled green peas
1 cup iceberg lettuce
2 tsp. vegetable bouillon
4 cups water
2 tsp. salt
2 tbs. freshly chopped parsley

To make the dough, combine the flours with the dried herbs, Delikata and Kurkuma powder, and mix to a firm but pliable dough with the egg and the oil. Shape into a roll and leave to rest beneath an up-turned dish for 30 minutes. • Peel the potatoes, scrape the carrots, wash and dice. Wash the lettuce, cut into quarters and then each quarter in 2–3 pieces. Fry the diced potato and carrot in butter with the peas for 2 or 3 minutes. Add the lettuce, water, and bouillon powder. Cook for about 10 minutes, then season with dried herbs. • For the pasta, bring the salted water to a boil. Grate the dough on a coarse grater, and bring the pieces of dough to boiling point. Strain the dough pieces through a sieve, and add to the soup with the parsley.

Turkey and Pasta Soup

Whole meal in itself, takes time

500 calories per serving
Preparation time: 1¾ hours

2 turkey wings (approx. 1¾ lbs.)
6 cups water
1 tsp. salt
1 bay leaf
5 white peppercorns
1 tsp. dried mixed herbs
¾ cup each carrots, broccoli, leeks and mushrooms
¼ cup butter
¾ cup wholemeal spaghetti rings
2 tsp. herb seasoning
2 tbs. freshly chopped parsley

Wash the turkey wings and cook with water, salt, bay leaf, peppercorns and dried herbs for 45 minutes. • Clean and wash the vegetables. Dice the carrots, break up the broccoli coarsely. Cut the leeks into rings and slice the mushrooms. • Remove the turkey wings from the stock, discard skin and bones, and chop the flesh into chunks. Sieve the broth. • Heat the butter in a pan and fry the vegetables for 1 or 2 minutes, stirring frequently. • Put the spaghetti rings into the soup, stir and cook for 5 minutes. • Add the meat and season the soup with the herb salt. • Garnish with parsley before serving.

Puszta Casserole

Complete meal

520 calories per serving
Preparation time: 1 hour

1¼ cups green peppers
2¼ cup beefsteak tomatoes
Topside of beef
Pinch freshly milled black pepper
2 onions
2 cloves garlic
1 small cup olive oil
4 cups hot water
1 bouquet garni
1 tbs. powdered vegetable bouillon
1 tsp. each mild paprika and cumin
½ tsp. dried thyme
½ cup wholemeal pasta (spirals)
2 pinches chili powder
1 tbs. each fresh chopped parsley and chives
¼ lb. Pecorino (ewes-milk) cheese

Quarter the green peppers, wash, discard seeds and pit, and cut into narrow strips. Peel the tomatoes and dice the flesh. Dice the meat and season with the pepper. • Peel and chop the onions and garlic, fry in olive oil and then remove with a straining spoon. Brown the meat in two batches in the oil until crisp. Add the onions, garlic and previously prepared vegetables and fry briefly. Put the water, bouillon powder, bouquet garni, paprika, cumin and thyme into the pan, and cook all together for 10 minutes, covered. • Place the pasta in the soup, and cook for about 8 minutes, uncovered. • Stir in the chili, parsley and chives. Do not allow the soup to cook any longer. Grate the cheese finely and sprinkle over the soup.

Wonton Soup

Takes time

220 calories per serving
Preparation time: 1¾ hours
Ingredients for 6 people

1¾ cups flour
1 egg
½ cup water
1 tsp. salt
2 scallions
½ cup canned bamboo shoots
¼ lb. chopped pork
¼ lb. chicken breast fillets
1 tbs. each soy sauce and sake (rice wine)
1 pinch each salt and freshly milled white pepper
1 egg white
3 qts. water
2 tsp. salt
4 cups chicken broth
1 handful watercress
Flour for the worktop

S ift the flour into a bowl. Add the beaten egg, water and salt and mix to a dough. Knead until smooth, then set aside to rest for an hour, covered. • Clean, wash and chop the scallions finely: place half of them in a dish. Chop the well-drained bamboo shoots into small pieces, and add to the scallions with the chopped pork. Finely chop the chicken breasts and add to the pork, with the soy sauce, the rice wine, salt and pepper and combine into a smooth stuffing. • Roll the dough out thinly onto a floured board and cut circles of 3 in. diameter and divide the filling between them. • Beat the egg-white with 1 tablespoon water, and paint the edges of the circles. Fold each circle in two, and press the edges together with a fork. Bring the salted water to a boil, and cook the wonton for 5 minutes, drain in a colander, and

set aside. • Heat the chicken broth; rinse, dry and chop the mustard and cress. Divide the wonton and the remaining scallions between six soup bowls, pour the chicken stock over, and garnish with watercress.

Wo-Mein Soup

Fast, very easy

430 calories per serving
Preparation time: 30 minutes

8 cups water
1 tsp. salt
1 cup Chinese egg noodles
9 oz. leg of pork
3 scallions
1¼ cups Chinese leaves
2 tbs. sesame seed oil
4 cups hot chicken broth
1 pinch each salt and pepper

B ring the salted water to a boil and cook the noodles for about 8 minutes, then drain and set aside. • Cut the pork into ¼ in. wide strips, and shred the cleaned scallions and Chinese leaves. • Fry the strips of meat until browned, add the onions and Chinese leaves, and continue cooking for 2 minutes. Add the noodles and pour the chicken broth over. • Season the soup with salt and pepper and serve in warmed soup bowls.

Nabeyaki-Udon Soup

Japanese specialty

260 calories per serving
Preparation time: 10 minutes

½ lb. chicken breast fillets
1 cup mushrooms
3 scallions
1 bunch parsley
4 cups chicken broth
⅔ cup Udon noodles or spaghetti
4 eggs
2 tbs. soy sauce

Cut the chicken breast fillets into strips ½ in. wide. Wipe the mushrooms, rinse, slice and set aside. Clean, and thoroughly wash the scallions, and cut into rings. Rinse and pat the parsley dry, remove the coarse stems, and chop the leaves finely. • Bring the chicken broth to a boil.

Half-cook the noodles in the broth (for about 3 minutes) and then add the chicken strips, mushrooms and rings of scallions. Cook 1 minute more. • Break the eggs one by one into a cup, and slide each one into the soup, rather like poaching eggs, and cook for 3 minutes. (The soup should be simmering very gently) Then carefully remove the eggs with a straining spoon and place in soup bowls or plates. • Flavor the soup with the soy sauce and stir in the parsley. Pour the soup over the eggs and serve immediately.

Takko Mein Soup

Chinese specialty, expensive

260 calories per serving
Preparation time: 40 minutes

6 dried Chinese mushrooms (Mu Err)
½ cup warm water
8 cups water
1 tsp. salt
1 tsp. oil
1 cup Chinese noodles
2 oz. lean raw ham
1¼ cups spinach
1¼ in. piece of fresh root ginger
4 cups chicken broth
1 can (½ lb.) oysters
1 pinch salt

Cover the dried mushrooms with warm water and leave to soak. • Bring the water to a boil with the salt and oil, and cook the noodles for 8 minutes, drain, set aside and cover to keep warm. • Cut the ham into strips, wash and dry the spinach and tear leaves into small pieces. Peel and finely grate the ginger root. • Drain the mushrooms and cut into shreds. Heat the chicken broth, and cook the ham strips for 5 minutes. Stir the spinach, mushrooms and oysters with can juice into the chicken broth. Cook the soup for 2 minutes. • Heat the noodles through in the soup, and stir in the ginger root. Finally, season the soup with salt.

Penne with Mushrooms and Tomatoes

Expensive, quick to make

430 calories per serving
Preparation time: 1 hour

2¼ cups mushrooms	
2¼ cups tomatoes	
1 large onion	
1 clove garlic	
4 tbs. olive oil	
10 cups water	
1 tsp. salt	
1¼ cups penne	
½ cup Pecorino (ewes milk) cheese	
Pinch each herb seasoning and freshly milled white pepper	
½ bunch basil	

Wash and dry the mushrooms, and cut in thin slices. Make a slit in the skin of the tomatoes at the bottom, dip briefly into boiling water, remove skins and central woody stalk. Dice the flesh. • Peel and chop the onion. Peel the garlic, cut into thin slices and fry until transparent in the oil with the chopped onions. • Add the mushrooms and cook, stirring, until the mushroom juice has evaporated completely. • Bring the salted water to a boil and cook the noodles until 'al dente', then strain in a colander and set aside, covered, to keep hot. • Stir the tomatoes into the mushroom sauce and cook for 8 minutes. • Grate the Pecorino. Season the sauce with herb seasoning and pepper. Strip the leaves from the sprigs of basil, wash, dry and stir into the sauce. Serve the noodles onto warm plates and divide the sauce over them, garnishing each portion with cheese.

Creamy Noodles with Nuts

Balkan specialty

760 calories per serving
Preparation time: 15 minutes
Cooking time: 20 minutes

10 cups water	
1 tsp. salt	
1¼ cups ribbon noodles (tagliatelle)	
1¾ cups shelled walnuts	
2 cloves garlic	
¼ cup butter	
1¼ cups sour cream	

Bring the salted water to a boil and barely cook the noodles: dried tagliatelle needs about 8 minutes, fresh takes only half as long. Grind ¾ cup walnuts in food mill (or processor), peel the garlic and slice thinly. •

Fry the ground walnuts and garlic quickly in butter in a large pan. • Drain the noodles and mix into the nuts and garlic mixture, seasoning with salt. • Place the noodles on a warmed dish, sprinkle the rest of the walnuts over them. • Stirring constantly, heat the sour cream very gently—do not allow to get hot—and serve separately.

Tip: For those who are not cautious about calories, this can be served with cream cheese rather than sour cream. There is also a sweet version of this recipe: instead of salt, flavor with honey or sugar—of course, in this case, omit the garlic!

Spaghetti with Chili Sauce

Really easy, economical

380 calories per serving
Preparation time: 1 hour

3 chilies	
1 green pepper	
2 onions	
1 clove garlic	
1 pinch salt	
1 small zucchini	
2 tomatoes	
2 tbs. olive oil	
6 oz. canned sweet corn	
2 tbs. tomato paste	
5 tbs. white wine	
1 pinch black pepper	
1 pinch dried oregano	
10 cups water	
1 tsp. salt	
1¼ cups spaghetti	

Halve the chilies and green pepper, discard the seeds and white pit, wash, dry and chop very finely. Peel and chop the onions, peel, chop, and crush the garlic with salt. Wash the zucchini, top and tail, and cut into chunks. Peel and quarter the tomatoes, discarding the stalky center; dice the flesh. • Heat 2 tablespoons oil in a saucepan and fry the onion until transparent. Mix in the prepared vegetables and the garlic, with the sweet corn, and cook over a low heat for 5 minutes. • Dilute the tomato paste with the wine, and mix into the vegetables. Season the sauce with pepper, oregano and salt. • Bring the salted water to a boil, add the remaining oil and the spaghetti, and cook for about 8 minutes, until 'al dente'. • Serve the spaghetti with sauce and freshly grated Parmesan cheese to taste.

Chicken Livers and Macaroni

Simple

330 calories per serving
Defrosting time: 30 minutes
Preparation time: 40 minutes

10 oz. frozen chicken livers
3 shallots
3 tbs. oil
1 tbs. flour
1 cup chicken broth
½ cup red wine
2 tsp. mild paprika
1 tsp. red wine vinegar
1 pinch each salt and freshly ground black pepper
10 cups water
1 tsp. salt
1¼ cups macaroni
3 tbs. cream

Remove the chicken livers from the packaging and allow to defrost, covered. • Rinse the livers, pat dry and cut into slices. • Peel the shallots, dice and fry until transparent in the oil. Add the sliced livers to the pan, and fry, stirring, with the flour, gradually adding the chicken broth and wine. Season the sauce with paprika, vinegar, salt and pepper, and cook for 5 minutes over a very low heat. Then increase the heat to evaporate some of the liquid. • Bring the salted water to a boil, and add the macaroni—do not cook too long, about 10 minutes, or it will be too soft—then drain. Blend the cream into the sauce and serve over the macaroni.

Spaghetti Con Aglio E Olio

A specialty, quick

310 calories per serving
Preparation time: 30 minutes

4 cloves garlic
1 bunch parsley
4 tbs. olive oil
1 tiny, hot red chili
10 cups water
1 tsp. salt
1 tbs. oil
1¼ cups spaghetti
4 tbs. freshly grated Pecorino (ewes milk cheese) or Parmesan cheese

Peel and chop the garlic finely. Wash and dry the parsley, and remove the coarse stalks; chop the leaves. • Heat the olive oil in a small pan and fry the garlic gently with the whole chili, stirring constantly. Take care not to burn the garlic, as it will then taste bitter. Remove the pan from the heat, cover and keep warm. • Bring the salted water to a boil, add the oil, and place the spaghetti into the rapidly boiling water for 8 minutes, until cooked but not too soft. • Drain the pasta in a colander. Discard the chili. • Mix the spaghetti with the garlic flavored oil in a previously well-warmed serving dish, and garnish with parsley. • Top with either 1 tablespoon of freshly grated Pecorino or Parmesan on each portion, according to taste.

Penne with Asparagus Tips

Easy, somewhat expensive

330 calories per serving
Preparation time: 45 minutes

14 oz. canned, peeled tomatoes
1 large clove garlic
3 anchovies
4½ cups green asparagus
3 tbs. olive oil
8 cups water
1½ tsp. salt
1 tsp. oil
½ cup penne (pasta quills)
1 pinch freshly milled white pepper

Drain the tomatoes in a colander, then chop coarsely. Peel the clove of garlic and cut in half lengthwise. Rinse the anchovies under cold water, dry and chop finely. • Thoroughly wash the asparagus under running warm water, and cut the upper green half of each spear into 1¼ in. pieces. (Use the remaining bottom parts for soup.) • Heat the oil in a large pan and let the garlic, anchovies, tomatoes and asparagus blend together in the hot oil, covered and over a moderate heat for 15 minutes. • Meanwhile, bring the water to a boil with 1 teaspoon salt and the oil. Put the pasta into the rapidly boiling water, stir once thoroughly and cook until 'al dente'–approx. 8 minutes. • Drain the pasta and keep warm, covered, in a heated serving dish. Season the vegetables with the salt and pepper and mix with the pasta. Leave the dish covered for 3 minutes for the ingredients to combine well.

Tagliatelle with Herbs

Takes time

310 calories per serving
Waiting time: 3 hours
Preparation time: 30 minutes

2¼ cups ripe tomatoes
2 cloves garlic
½ large onion
1 stick celery
1 bunch each basil and parsley
3 tbs. cold-pressed olive oil (virgin oil)
1 tsp. fresh oregano, or ½ tsp. dried
½ tsp. salt
1 pinch freshly milled black pepper
8 cups water
1 tsp. salt
1 cup tagliatelle
1 tsp. oil

Score around the skins of the tomatoes at the bottom, immerse briefly in boiling water, peel, dice the flesh and discard the seeds and stalky center part. Allow to drain in a colander. Peel the garlic and use a garlic press to crush into a large serving dish. Peel and finely chop the onions. Wash and dry the celery, remove the coarse stringy parts, and chop the rest. Wash the basil and parsley, pat dry, chop finely and mix with the tomato pieces, the onion and celery dice, the oil, and the fresh or dried oregano. Season the vegetable mixture with salt and pepper and leave in refrigerator for 3 hours. • Cook the tagliatelle in boiling salted water with the oil for about 8 minutes, or until the pasta is 'al dente', then drain well, and serve immediately with the tomato and herb mixture.

Pasta Shells with Zucchini

Quick, economical

290 calories per serving
Preparation time: 35 minutes

3 cloves garlic
1 bunch parsley
3 medium firm zucchinis
3 tbs. olive oil
1 tsp. fresh oregano or ½ tsp. dried
1½ tsp. salt
1 pinch freshly milled black pepper
1 tsp. oil
8 cups water
1 cup pasta shells

Peel the garlic, wash and dry the parsley: chop both finely. Wash, dry and slice the zucchini. • Fry the garlic in oil, add the zucchini, fry until golden and flavor to taste with oregano, parsley, ½ teaspoon salt and the pepper. Keep the vegetables warm. • Add the rest of the salt and the oil to the water, and bring to a boil. Cook the pasta for about 8 minutes, until cooked but not too soft, then drain well in a colander. • Mix the pasta shells with the vegetables and heat through.

Home-Made Tagliatelle with Spinach

Takes time

400 calories per serving
Preparation time: 1½ hours

1¾ cups flour
2 eggs
½ tsp. salt
3 cups tender spinach
2 cloves garlic
1 tbs. oil
2 tbs. butter
1 tsp. salt
1 pinch freshly grated nutmeg
1 pinch freshly milled black pepper
3 qts. water
1 tsp. salt
¼ cup freshly grated Parmesan cheese
Flour for the work surface

Make a firm, pliable dough from the flour, eggs and salt; shape dough into a roll and leave to rest under an upturned dish for 1 hour. • Clean the spinach and steam gently in its own juice. Leave it to cook, then chop finely. • Peel and halve the garlic cloves. Heat the oil and 1 tablespoon butter in a saucepan, fry the garlic until brown, and remove from the oil. Place the spinach into the oil, with the salt, nutmeg and pepper and cook, covered, for 5 minutes over a very low heat. • Roll out the dough thinly on a floured work surface, roll up, and cut into strips, which can be spread out on the work surface to dry briefly. • Bring the salted water to a boil. Cook the tagliatelle in the rapidly boiling water for 5 minutes, or until 'al dente', drain in a colander and mix with the remaining butter in a heated serving dish. • Spread the spinach over the pasta and sprinkle Parmesan on top.

Tagliatelle with Tomatoes and Mushrooms

Italian specialty

310 calories per serving
Preparation time: 1 hour

1 large white onion
2 cloves garlic
2¾ cups mushrooms
1 tbs. lemon juice
2 beefsteak tomatoes
2 tbs. butter
1 pinch each of salt, sugar and black pepper
8 cups water
1 tsp. salt
1 tsp. oil
1 cup tagliatelle
½ bunch sage

Peel and chop the onion. Peel and chop the garlic very finely. Clean the mushrooms, slice vertically and sprinkle with lemon juice. Score around the tomato skins, dip into boiling water, skin, quarter, discard the center stalky part, and dice the flesh. • Heat the butter, and fry the chopped onion until transparent. • Add the mushrooms and the garlic, and cook over low heat for 10 minutes. • Mix the tomatoes into the mushrooms. Season the vegetables with salt, sugar and pepper. • Bring the salted water to a boil, and add the oil. Cook the tagliatelle for 8 minutes (they should not be too soft). • Rip the sage leaves from the stalk, wash, dry and shred. • Rinse the pasta in a colander, and leave to drain, before mixing with the vegetables. Sprinkle the sage on top. • Serve the pasta immediately in a previously warmed dish. Sprinkle with grated Parmesan cheese.

Pasta Nests with Mussel Sauce

Simple

360 calories per serving
Preparation time: 40 minutes

10 cups water
1½ tsp. salt
4 nests of tagliatelle, each about 2½ oz.
7 oz. canned or bottled mussels
5 anchovies
2 tbs. capers
1 tbs. cornstarch
1 tsp. hot mustard
1 pinch each salt and black pepper
A few drops lemon juice
4 tbs. cream

Bring the salted water to a boil, and place the pasta nests in the saucepan, turning down the heat a little, so that the pasta cooks in about 8 minutes. Then drain the tagliatelle in a sieve, reserving the water. Keep the pasta covered and hot. • Drain the mussels and reserve the juice. Chop the anchovies very finely and mix with the drained capers and the mussels. • Mix the cornstarch with the liquid from the mussels. Bring 2 cups of pasta cooking liquid to a boil again, and mix with the cornstarch paste, bring to a boil once and remove from the heat. Add the mustard, salt, pepper and lemon juice to the sauce, blend in the mussels and the cream, and reheat; do not boil though. • Serve the pasta nests individually with the mussel sauce.

Elbow Pasta with Broccoli

Very simple

330 calories per serving
Preparation time: 1 hour

3 cloves garlic
3 anchovies
4½ cups broccoli
8 cups water
1 tsp. salt
1 cup elbow pasta
3 tbs. olive oil
1 pinch cayenne pepper

Peel the garlic and chop finely. Rinse the anchovies, dry and chop. Wash the broccoli thoroughly and drain well. Trim the stalks and cut the broccoli into 2 in. pieces (chop thicker pieces shorter, so that the cooking time is the same). • Bring the salted water to a boil, and cook the broccoli, covered, over moderate heat for about 15 minutes, then drain in a colander, reserving the cooking liquid. Keep the vegetables warm. • Cook the elbow pasta in the reserved broccoli cooking water for approx. 8 minutes, until 'al dente'. • Meanwhile, heat the olive oil in a small saucepan. Let the garlic, anchovies and cayenne pepper fry gently over low heat for 15 minutes, stirring. • Drain the pasta in a colander, place in a preheated serving dish, mix with broccoli and the anchovy sauce and allow to stand for 5 minutes, for the flavors to mingle. Mix once more before serving. • This dish is better with freshly ground white pepper to taste.

Tomatoes and Gnocchi

A good accompaniment

400 calories per serving
Drying time: 2 days
Preparation time: 50 minutes

2½ cups flour
½ tsp. salt
1 pinch saffron
3½ cups beefsteak tomatoes
3 cloves garlic
3 tbs. olive oil
1½ tbs. chopped basil
1 pinch white pepper
1 tsp. freshly chopped oregano
3 qts. water
1½ tsp. salt
2 tbs. freshly grated Pecorino (ewes-milk) cheese

Sift the flour into a bowl and add the salt. Soak the saffron in a little water and add to the flour. Gradually add the water to form a dough. Knead the dough well, shape into ropes ½ in. thick, and cut the ropes into pieces 2 in. long. Score around the bottom of the tomatoes, and dip into boiling water, skin, chop up and discard the hard core. Peel and quarter the garlic. • Heat the oil in a large saucepan, fry the garlic, stirring, and then discard. Add the basil, the tomatoes, the salt and pepper to the oil. Stir well and cook gently for 30 minutes. Lastly, mix in the oregano. • To cook the gnocchi, bring the salted water to a boil. Cook the gnocchi until they rise to the surface, then drain and serve in a heated dish with the tomatoes. Sprinkle with cheese.

Potato Gnocchi

A good accompaniment, lengthy cooking time

810 calories per serving
Preparation time: 1¼ hours

4½ potatoes
1 tsp. salt
1¼ cups Parmesan cheese
1¼ cups flour
4 qts. water
2 tsp. salt
¾ cup butter

Peel the potatoes, wash and cut into even, large pieces: cook in salted water, covered, for 20 minutes. • Grate the Parmesan cheese. Sieve (or use food processor) the cooked potatoes onto a floured board, and leave to cool. Season with a little salt, and knead into the potatoes as much flour as it takes to pro-duce a smooth, but not too firm, dough. Leave the potato dough to rest for 10 minutes, then divide into 8 portions, and shape these into rolls as thick as a thumb. Cut them into 1 in. lengths, and press lightly with a fork, to make a faint pattern. • Bring the salted water to a boil in a large saucepan. Carefully slide the gnocchi in, and stir gently with a fork. When the gnocchi rise to the surface, they are cooked. Remove with a straining spoon and drain. Butter a well warmed serving dish thickly, and layer the gnocchi with grated Parmesan cheese and the rest of the butter. • Serve the gnocchi hot.

Cornmeal Gnocchi

Suitable for an accompaniment, takes time

760 calories per serving
Preparation time: 1 hour

5 cups water
1 tbs. salt
2½ cups cornmeal, not too fine
1 cup Parmesan cheese
½ cup melted butter
1 cup cream (8 oz.)
Butter to grease baking dish

Bring the salted water to a boil in a deep pan. Gradu-ally add the cornmeal and beat with an egg whisk to separate the grains, and avoid lumps. Cook over low heat for 45 minutes, by which time it should be like a thick porridge consistency. • Meanwhile grate the Parmesan and butter a shallow gratin dish generously. Preheat the oven to 400°F. • Using a tablespoon repeatedly dipped in hot water, shape gnocchi from the cornmeal, and gently slide into the au gratin dish. Cover the first layer of gnocchi with Parmesan, and the second with melted butter. Pour the cream over the final layer. • Bake the cornmeal gnocchi in the oven for 5 minutes.

Fettucine with Garlic Butter

Quick, economical

470 calories per serving
Preparation time: 35 minutes

10 cups water
1½ tsp. salt
1¼ cups fettucine
¼ cup butter
2 tbs. pine nuts
¼ cup Pecorino (ewes-milk) cheese
2 cloves garlic
1 pinch herb seasoning

Bring the water to a boil and add the salt. Cook the fettucine approx. 8 minutes until 'al dente'. • Melt 1 teaspoon butter in a small saucepan, and brown the pine nuts lightly. Grate the cheese, peel the garlic, chop and mix with the herb seasoning, and crush. Blend the garlic into the remaining butter. • Mix the well-drained pasta well with the butter, and place in a heated serving dish. • Sprinkle the toasted pine nuts over the pasta. Garnish the pasta with the grated cheese and serve immediately.

Tip: Instead of pine nuts, chopped walnuts are also very tasty. Parmesan may be substituted for Pecorino cheese.

Fettucine with Lecso

Quick, economical

470 calories per serving
Preparation time: 35 minutes
Cooking time: 20 minutes

2¼ cups yellow peppers (capsicums)
1¼ cups tomatoes
2 large white onions
1 chili
2 oz. lean bacon
3 tbs. sunflower oil
10 cups water
1½ tsp. salt
1¼ cups fettucine
¼ cup freshly grated Parmesan cheese

Wash the yellow peppers, halve, remove center core, white stalky parts and seeds. Cut into narrow strips. Score around the skin at the bottom of the tomatoes, and dip them briefly in boiling water, remove skins and stalky part in middle, and dice the flesh. Peel and finely chop the onions. Wash the chili and slice into narrow rings. Dice the bacon. • Heat the oil in a pan, and brown the bacon until crispy. Add the onions and fry until transparent, stirring, and then the pepper, tomato, and chili. Leave the vegetables to steam in their own juice gently for 15 minutes. • Bring the water to a boil, add the salt and the fettucine, and cook until 'al dente', then strain and set aside. • Season the Lecso sauce, serve the pasta on a preheated dish. Top with the sauce and Parmesan cheese before serving.

Hah Gavs

Chinese specialty, complicated

310 calories per serving
Preparation time: 1¾ hours

| 1 cup water |
| 1¼ cups flour |
| 5 canned water chestnuts |
| ½ bunch parsley |
| 1 oz. lean raw ham |
| 6 oz. shrimps |
| 1 pinch salt |
| ½ tsp. sugar |
| 4 tbs. sesame seed oil |
| 8 tbs. soy sauce |

Bring the water to a boil. Sift the flour into a bowl, and stir in the boiling water, and make a pliable dough. Shape into a roll 1¼ in. thick and leave to rest covered by a cloth for an hour. • Drain the water chestnuts and cut into very small pieces. Wash and pat dry the parsley, remove the coarse stem and chop the leaves finely. Chop the ham and shrimps. Mix all the chopped ingredients together and season with salt and sugar. • Cut pieces of dough the size of a walnut from the roll, shape into balls in the palm of the hand and flatten. Place the stuffing in the center, make each circle into a little "pouch" and press the edges together. • In a large shallow pan bring 2 in. water to a boil. Oil a plate, and place the "pouches" on it, and set it, supported on two teacups in the pan of boiling water, so that the "pouches" can steam for 10 minutes. • Mix the soy sauce with the remaining sesame seed oil and offer as an accompaniment to the "pouches".

Jao Mais

Chinese specialty, a bit expensive

500 calories per serving
Preparation time: 1¾ hours

| 3 dried Chinese mushrooms (Mu Err) |
| 2½ cups flour |
| 1 egg |
| ½ cup water |
| ½ tsp. salt |
| 7 oz. shrimps |
| 7 oz. chopped pork |
| ½ tsp. each salt and pepper |
| 1 pinch freshly milled white pepper |
| 4 tbs. sake (rice wine) |
| 4 tbs. sesame seed oil |
| 4 tbs. soy sauce |
| Flour for the workboard |

Leave the mushrooms to soak in lukewarm water. • Sift the flour into a bowl. Beat the egg with the water and salt, add to the flour, and make a pliable dough. Leave to rest covered by a cloth for an hour. • Chop the shrimps and the drained mushrooms finely, and mix with the chopped pork, salt, sugar, pepper and sake. • Shape the dough into a roll approx. 1¼ in. thick, and divide into 40 small balls. Roll the balls out very thinly and dust with flour. • Divide the filling among the circles of dough. Wet the edges and fold the circles into crescent shapes, pressing the edges together. Place the "pouches" on an oiled plate, and as described in Hah Gavs, steam for 15 minutes. • Mix the soy sauce with the remaining sesame seed oil and offer as an accompaniment to the "pouches".

Won Tons

Chinese specialty, a bit expensive

810 calories per serving
Preparation time: 2½ hours

2¼ cups flour
1 egg
½ cup water
½ tsp. salt
1 scallion
½ cup canned bamboo shoots
10 oz. ground pork
1 tbs. soy sauce
1 tbs. sake (rice wine) or dry sherry
1 pinch each salt and freshly milled white pepper
1 egg white
1 large cup canned drained plums, without pits
1 pinch each cinnamon and grated lemon peel
Flour for the workboard

To fry: 4 cups oil or 2 cups coconut oil

Sift the flour into a bowl. Beat the egg with the water and salt, add to the flour, and make a pliable dough; knead until elastic and smooth–this takes 10 to 15 minutes. Leave to rest covered by an upturned dish or cloth for an hour. • Wash the scallion thoroughly, dry and cut into thin rings. Cut the bamboo shoots into ⅛ in. pieces. Mix the pork with the soy sauce, the rice wine or sherry, the salt and pepper, and then combine the scallions and bamboo shoots. • Shape the pasta dough into 1¼ in. thick roll and cut 40 pieces from it. Shape into balls and then roll each out on a floured board very thinly, and dust with flour. Beat the egg white and 1 tablespoon water together and paint the edges of the circles, di-

vide the filling between the circles, and fold them together into crescent shapes, pressing the edges together firmly with a fork. Leave the rest until the plum sauce is ready. • Purée or chop finely the plum jam with the cinnamon and grated lemon rind in the blender, and pass through a sieve. Sweeten the sauce to taste and thin with some of the remaining juice. • Heat the oil or coconut butter in a frying pan, or deep fryer, to 350°F, and fry the pouches of dough in portions in the oil on both sides until golden. Turn the pasta during cooking. • Serve the pasta either hot or cold with the plum sauce.

Tip: To avoid drying out the dough slices too quickly after rolling, fill and seal them in batches, covering the remaining pasta circles with a damp cloth. If the pasta is too dry, it will not

fold over the filling as well as it should. Bamboo shoots are also rather soggy. Instead use finely chopped bean sprouts mixed into the stuffing.

Kuo Tiehs

Takes time

550 calories per serving
Preparation time: 2 hours

2½ cups flour
1 cup water
1 cup Chinese leaves
2 scallions
9 oz. chopped pork
2 tbs. soy sauce
1 tbs. rice wine
½ tsp. each salt and sugar
6 tbs. oil
Flour for the workboard

Place half the flour in a bowl. Bring ½ cup water to a boil, stir ½ cup cold water into half the flour, and mix the boiling water with the other half of the flour. Knead both doughs together and leave to rest covered, while preparing the filling. • Wash the Chinese leaves, shred, and cook with 4 tablespoons water in a covered saucepan over a low heat for 10 minutes. • Clean the scallions and cut into thin rings; mix with the minced pork, the soy sauce, rice wine, salt, sugar and the Chinese leaves. • Shape the dough into a 1¼ in. thick roll, cut walnut-sized pieces off, and roll out thinly on floured surface. • Divide the filling between the circles of dough. Gather the dough circles around the filling like small drawstring bags, and leave to rest covered with a cloth on a floured board for 20 minutes. • Heat half the oil in a pan, and place the pasta 'bags' in the pan. Add enough cold water to come halfway up the 'bags', and steam for 3 minutes in the covered pan. Then drain off the liquid. Trickle the remaining oil over the 'bags' and cook until crisp for 10–12 minutes. • Serve with Chinese mustard, soy or duck sauce.

Pasta with Sauces or Ragoûts

Spaghetti with Gorgonzola Sauce

Quite expensive, simple to make

1000 calories per serving
Preparation time: 30 minutes

1 small onion
1–2 cloves garlic
3 tbs. olive oil
1 tsp. flour
2 cups cream
½ cup dry white wine
1¼ cups gorgonzola cheese
¼ cup pine nuts
1¾ cup spaghetti
4 qts. water
2 tsp. salt
½ tsp. Italian-style dried herbs

Peel and chop the onion and garlic very finely and fry quickly in oil. Shake the flour over, and make a sauce with the cream and white wine. • Stir 1¼ cups Gorgonzola and the pine nuts into the sauce, and heat for 10 minutes. • Place the spaghetti in boiling salted water until just cooked but not soft, drain, and mix with the sauce and the herbs. Sprinkle the remaining gorgonzola, broken up small, over the top and serve.

Spaghetti with Creamy Salmon Sauce

Rather expensive

1000 calories per serving
Preparation time: 45 minutes

½ cup dry white wine
½ tsp. salt and peppercorns
½ bunch tarragon
12 oz. fresh salmon
2 cups cream
¾ cup carrots
1¾ cups spaghetti

4 qts. water
2 tsp. salt
1 tbs. oil
1 pinch white pepper
1 tbs. butter straight from the refrigerator

Bring the wine to a boil with the salt, peppercorns and 1 sprig tarragon, and poach the salmon in this for 3–5 minutes, before flaking. • Strain the stock through a sieve and boil down to half the quantity. • Add the cream over a higher heat and re-duce again to half the quantity. • Scrape the carrots and slice thinly; blanch for 2 minutes. • Cook the spaghetti in the salted water and oil until 'al dente'. • Finely chop the remaining tar-ragon, and mix into the cream sauce, season with salt and pep-per. Add the butter a teaspoon at a time. Briefly heat the salmon and the carrots in the sauce.

Spaghetti with Basil Sauce

Very easy, quick

710 calories per serving
Preparation time: 30 minutes

2 shallots
1–2 cloves garlic
2 tbs. olive oil
2¼ cups cream
2 bunches basil
1 pinch each salt and freshly milled white pepper
1–2 tsp. lemon juice
1 egg yolk
1¾ cups spaghetti

Fry the finely chopped shal-lots and garlic in the oil, and make a sauce with the cream. Stir in the chopped basil, spices and egg yolk. Combine the sauce with the cooked pasta.

Wholewheat Spaghetti with Tofu Sauce

Complete meal, easy

710 calories per serving
Preparation time: 1 hour

1¼ cups tofu (bean curd)
2 tbs. soy sauce
3 tbs. sesame seeds
1 pinch freshly milled black pepper
2¼ cups tomatoes
1 onion
2¼ cups cucumber
¼ cup butter
4 qts. water
2 tsp. salt
1¾ cups wholewheat spaghetti
½ cup Pecorino (ewes-milk) cheese
1 carton sour cream (8 oz.)
4 tbs. fresh dill, finely chopped
1 tsp. mild paprika

Drain the tofu, cut into ¼ in. cubes, and mix in a small bowl with the soy sauce, the sesame seeds and the pepper. • Slit around the tomato skins and dip in boiling water; peel and remove the stalky center. Dice the flesh. Peel the cucumber and dice. • Peel the onion, finely dice and fry until transparent in the butter. Add the tofu mixture and fry 2–3 minutes, turning. Add the cucumber and tomatoes to the tofu and cook together over a low heat for 10–15 minutes. • Bring the water to a boil, add salt and spaghetti. Cook until 'al dente' then drain in a colander, rinse briefly with cold water and keep hot in a previously warmed serving dish.
• Grate the Pecorino cheese.
• Remove the ragout from the heat, mix in the cheese, sour cream and dill. Season with the paprika and a little more soy sauce. • Serve the sauce on top of the spaghetti.

Pasta Casserole with Mushrooms

Easy

620 calories per serving
Preparation time: 40 minutes

2½ cups mushrooms
2 tbs. butter
1 pinch each salt and black pepper
2 tsp. mild paprika
3 tbs. tomato paste
1 carton fresh cream (8 oz.)
4 qts. water
2 tsp. salt
1¾ cups elbow macaroni
½ bunch parsley

Rinse the mushrooms with cold water, pat dry and cut up. • Heat the butter in a pan, fry the mushrooms with the salt, pepper and paprika. Stir the tomato paste into the cream and mix both into the mushrooms. Leave the mushrooms to simmer on low heat until the pasta is cooked. • Bring the salted water to a boil and drop in the pasta to cook for eight minutes.
• Drain the cooked pasta in a colander and mix with the mushrooms in a heated serving dish, sprinkled with chopped parsley.
• Serve with grated Parmesan cheese.

Tip: As pasta should always be served hot, it is a good idea to keep the mushroom mixture hot in a double-boiler and to heat the serving dish well.

Pasta with Ham Sauce

Economical, easy to make

720 calories per serving
Preparation time: 30 minutes

¼ lb. cooked lean ham
4 shallots
1 clove garlic
2 tbs. butter
½ cup hot beef broth
1 carton cream (6 oz.)
4 qts. water
2 tsp. salt
1¾ cups pasta twists
1 egg yolk
1 bunch chives

Cut the ham into very fine strips; peel and finely chop the shallots and garlic. • Melt the butter, and fry the shallots and garlic until transparent, adding the ham. Pour in the meat stock and let it all cook together. Stir in the cream and leave the liquid to reduce, uncovered, while the pasta cooks. • Bring the salted water to a boil, and cook the pasta until 'al dente'. Beat the egg yolk with 2 tbs. hot sauce, and then blend into the cream sauce. Do not allow to return to a boil. Wash, dry and chop the chives. • Drain the pasta in a colander, mix into the cream sauce and serve in a previously heated dish, strewn with chives. • A tasty dressed tomato salad with mozzarella cheese, onion rings and fresh basil goes very well with this.

Spaghetti with Anchovies

Italian specialty

520 calories per serving
Preparation time: 1 hour

5 anchovies
1¼ cup ripe beef steak tomatoes
½ bunch parsley
¼ cup black olives
2–3 cloves garlic
1 tbs. capers
1 pinch salt
½ tsp. fresh or 1 pinch dried oregano
1 pinch chili powder (hot) or cayenne
1¾ cups spaghetti
4 qts. water
1 tsp. salt

Rinse the anchovies, where necessary, dry and finely chop. Slit the tomatoes around the bottom, and briefly dip into boiling water. Remove skins and the stalky center. Chop the tomato flesh. Wash and dry the parsley, and chop, along with the pitted olives, peeled garlic and the drained capers. • Heat the oil and stir-fry the anchovies, parsley, olives, garlic and capers for about 5 minutes, and then add tomatoes. Season with salt, oregano and chili or cayenne. Leave the sauce to thicken over a medium heat for 30 minutes. • Cook the spaghetti in swiftly boiling water about 8 minutes, until just firm to the bite. • Mix the drained spaghetti with the sauce.

Wholemeal Pasta with Veal Ragout

Whole meal recipe

580 calories per serving
Marinading time: 1 hour
Preparation time: 1¼ hour

1 lb. 2 oz. shoulder veal
2 tbs. soy sauce
2 pinches white pepper
1 onion
1 bay leaf
2 cloves
2¼ cups each zucchini and tomatoes
1 tbs. melted butter
1¼ cups green wholemeal pasta
3 qts. water
1½ tsp. salt
1 tbs. wheatmeal
½ carton cream (4 oz.)
½ tsp. each freshly chopped rosemary, marjoram and basil
2 tsp. freshly chopped lemon balm mint or parsley

Cut the meat into 1 in. cubes, mix with soy sauce and 1 pinch pepper and leave to marinade for 1 hour. • Briefly, sauté the onion, the bay leaf and the cloves in the butter. Clean the zucchini, top and tail and chop coarsely. Skin the tomatoes and quarter, discarding the stalky centers. • Fry the meat in the butter for 5 minutes, then add the rest of the vegetables with the pepper, and cook for 1 hour. • Cook the pasta in swiftly boiling salted water for about 10 minutes. • Stir the flour into the cream, blend into the ragout and leave to cook for 2 more minutes. Discard the onion and mix in the herbs. • Drain the pasta in a colander and serve with the ragout on top.

Babuschka-Pasta with Chinese Leaves

A complete meal in itself

640 calories per serving
Preparation time: 1 hour

1½ cups wholemeal flour
1¼ cups buckwheat flour
½ tsp. sea salt
3 tbs. sunflower oil
1 cup lukewarm water
¼ cup sunflower seeds
3 cooking apples
2¼ cups Chinese leaves
10 cups water
1 tsp. salt
2 tbs. butter
½ cup cream
1 tsp. each herb seasoning and mild paprika
1 tsp. honey
2 tbs. freshly chopped parsley

To make the pasta, mix all the flour with the salt, oil and water to a smooth but firm dough. Invert a warmed dish over it. • Toast the sunflower seeds in a pan. Wash, peel, quarter, core and dice the apples and place in a saucepan with 1 cup water. Clean and finely shred the Chinese leaves finely, add to the apples and cook for 15–20 minutes. • Roll out the pasta dough in 4 portions to the thickness of a knife, and cut into strips ½ in. wide. Leave the pasta to dry for 5 minutes, then cook in swiftly boiling salted water; it is cooked when it rises to the surface. Drain the pasta and mix with the butter and sunflower seeds. • Stir the spices, the honey and the parsley into the cream, and combine with the vegetables gently.

Farfalle with Sovritosauce

Quick, economical

520 calories per serving
Preparation time: 45 minutes

| 1 thin strip of fatty bacon |
| 2 oz. back bacon |
| 3 shallots |
| 1 small green pepper |
| 1 beefsteak tomato |
| 1 clove garlic |
| ½ cup beef broth |
| 1¾ cups farfalle (pasta bows) |
| 4 qts. water |
| 2 tsp. salt |
| 8 black olives |
| 1 pinch cayenne pepper |
| 1 pinch dried thyme |

Shred all the bacon and fry. Peel the shallots, finely chop and sauté in the bacon fat until transparent. Halve the pepper,

discard the central core, the pit, seeds, etc., and dice. Slit the tomatoes, dip into boiling water briefly, remove the skins, and stalky center, and dice the flesh. Peel and finely chop the garlic, and add with the diced green pepper and the tomato to the bacon and onion mixture. Pour the meat stock over and cook the vegetables for 10–15 minutes. • Cook the pasta for 8 minutes in salted water, until 'al dente'. Halve and pit the olives, mix into the vegetable sauce and season with salt, cayenne and thyme. • Serve the sauce on top of the noodles on a preheated serving plate.

Spaghetti Bolognese

Italian specialty, a classic recipe

930 calories per serving
Preparation time: 10 minutes

¼ lb. bacon
2 onions
1 carrot
3 sticks celery
1 bunch parsley
3 tbs. olive oil
10 oz. ground beef
4 oz. ground pork
2 tbs. tomato paste
1¼ cups hot beef broth
2 cups dry white wine
1 bay leaf
½ tsp. salt
1 pinch black pepper
1 pinch sugar
4 qts. water
2 tsp. salt
1¾ cups spaghetti
4 oz. chicken livers
2 tsp. butter

Cut the bacon into narrow strips, peel and finely chop the onions, scrape, wash and dice the carrots. Wash the celery and finely slice. Wash, pat dry and chop the parsley. • Heat 2 tbs. oil in a large saucepan. Brown the ground meat, stirring, add the bacon and onions and brown for 3 more minutes. • Add the carrot, celery, parsley, tomato paste, stock, wine, bay leaf, salt, pepper and sugar. Cook the sauce gently for 30 minutes over a low heat. • Bring the water to a boil, and add the salt, the remaining oil and the spaghetti—cook until 'al dente', about 8 minutes. • Fry the chicken livers in 1 tsp. butter, finely chop and add to the sauce. Drain the spaghetti in a colander, add the rest of the butter and serve with sauce on top.

Pasta with Basil Sauce (Pesto)

Italian specialty, classic recipe

810 calories per serving
Preparation time: 30 minutes

| 2 bunches basil |
| 2–3 cloves garlic |
| 1 tbs. pine nuts |
| 1 pinch salt |
| ½ cup freshly grated Parmesan cheese |
| 1 cup olive oil |
| 4 qts. water |
| 2 tsp. salt |
| 1¾ cups pasta (spaghetti, macaroni or fettucine) |
| 1 tbs. butter |

Wash the basil and strip the leaves from the stems. Peel and coarsely chop the garlic, and crush to a paste with the basil, pine nuts and salt. Add the Parmesan. Add the oil, at first drop by drop, but then in a steady stream, stirring it into the paste. • Bring the water to a boil and add pasta and salt, cook until 'al dente', drain and rinse with warm water. Mix in the butter, and serve the pasta. Serve the pesto separately.

Pasta with Salsa Di Pomodori

Italian specialty

600 calories per serving
Preparation time: 50 minutes

| 4½ cups very ripe tomatoes |
| 2 medium onions |
| 2 tbs. olive oil |
| 1 bunch basil |
| 2 tbs. tomato paste |
| 1 tsp. sugar |
| ½ tsp. salt |
| 1 pinch freshly milled black pepper |
| 4 qts. water |
| 2 tsp. salt |
| 1¾ cups pasta (spaghetti, macaroni or fettuccine) |
| 1 tsp. butter |
| ½ cup freshly grated or Parmesan cheese |

Wash the tomatoes, discard the stalks, and chop up into small pieces. Peel and finely chop the onions and fry in the oil until transparent. Add the tomatoes and cook, covered, for 10 minutes. • Wash the basil and strip the leaves from the stems. Set aside some leaves to garnish the dish, but chop the rest and add to the onions and tomatoes. Cook the pasta about 8 minutes, until 'al dente'. • Meanwhile, heat the olive oil in a small saucepan. Let the garlic, anchovies and cayenne pepper fry gently over a low heat for 15 minutes, stirring. • Drain the pasta in a colander, place in a preheated serving dish, mix with broccoli and the anchovy sauce and allow to stand for 5 minutes, for the flavors to mingle. Mix once more before serving. • This dish is better with freshly ground white pepper to taste.

Pasta with Tuna Fish Sauce

Quick, economical

500 calories per serving
Preparation time: 30 minutes

2 cloves garlic
10 oz. canned tuna
1¾ cups tomatoes
1 tbs. olive oil
½ tsp. salt
3 qts. water
1½ tsp. salt
1 tbs. oil
1¼ cups fettucine
1 bunch parsley
A few basil leaves

Peel and finely chop the garlic. Drain and flake the tuna fish. • Slit around the tomato skins at the rounded end, submerge in boiling water, allow to cool and remove the skins, and cut away the hard stalky center. • Heat the olive oil and fry the garlic until golden. Add the pieces of tomato, the tuna fish, and salt and cook covered for 20 minutes over a very low heat. • Bring the water to a boil with the salt and oil. Throw the noodles into the swiftly boiling water, stir thoroughly once, and cook until 'al dente'. • Wash the parsley, dry, discard the coarse stems and chop the leaves, mix into the tuna sauce.
• Drain the pasta, then place in a preheated dish and cover with the tuna sauce; garnish with the basil leaves.

Tagliatelle Alla Emilia-Romagna

Very simple, Italian specialty

450 calories per serving
Preparation time: 40 minutes

2 oz. lean bacon
3 qts. water
1½ tsp. oil
1¼ cups fettucine
1 tbs. oil
4 tbs. cream
1¼ cups frozen peas

Dice the bacon. Bring the water to a boil, add oil, salt and pasta, stir thoroughly once and cook until 'al dente'. Fill a serving dish with very hot water.
• Heat the oil in a pan and brown the bacon until crispy. Add the cream and frozen peas, stir and cook over a low heat for 5 minutes. • Drain the pasta in a colander, and mix with the peas in the preheated serving dish.

Spaghetti Alla Carbonara

Italian specialty, economical

600 calories per serving
Preparation time: 30 minutes

3 qts. water
1½ tsp. salt
1 tbs. oil
1¾ cups spaghetti
2 oz. lean bacon
¼ cup Pecorino (ewes-milk) cheese
2 cloves garlic
1 tbs. olive oil
2 eggs
4 tbs. cream
½ tsp. salt
1 pinch white pepper

Bring the water to a boil, and add salt, oil and spaghetti. Cook for 8 minutes until 'al dente'. • Dice the bacon, peel and quarter the garlic. • Heat the olive oil in a large pan, and brown the garlic, stirring frequently; then discard the garlic. Fry the bacon until crispy and brown. • Mix the eggs with cream, cheese, salt and pepper in a preheated dish. Drain the spaghetti, add to the bacon in the pan, heat once more, stirring, and mix with the egg and cream mixture in the serving dish.

Tip: To make this recipe even better, use 2 egg yolks with the cream and cheese.

Spaghetti Alla Napoletana

Economical, Neapolitan specialty

520 calories per serving
Preparation time: 40 minutes

1 onion
1 tbs. olive oil
1 sprig each parsley and basil
1¾ cups tomatoes
1 pinch paprika
2½ tsp. sugar
3 qts. water
1 tsp. oil
1¾ cups spaghetti
¼ cup Parmesan cheese

Peel and finely chop the onion and fry in the oil until golden. Wash the herbs, dry, remove coarse stems and chop. Add to the onions. • Slit the tomato skins, immerse in boiling water, peel and dice, removing the stalk and hard center. Add tomatoes to the onions, with the paprika, ½ tsp. salt and sugar. Cover and cook over low heat for 10 minutes. • Cook the spaghetti for 8 minutes until 'al dente' in fast boiling water with salt and oil. Grate the Parmesan. Serve the drained spaghetti in a preheated serving dish mixed with the tomato sauce. • Serve the Parmesan cheese separately.

Stufatu

Takes time to cook

640 calories per serving
Preparation time: 2½ hours
Ingredients for 6 people

10 oz. lean stewing beef
10 oz. lean loin of pork
2 oz. bacon
3 large beefsteak tomatoes
1 large onion
4 cloves garlic
4 tbs. olive oil
½ cup dry white wine
1 tsp. salt
2 pinches white pepper
3 qts. water
1½ tsp. salt
2¼ cups macaroni
¼ cup freshly grated Gruyere cheese
2 tbs. chopped parsley

Cube the meat, removing fat and sinews, cut the bacon into strips. Peel the tomatoes and cut into small pieces. • Peel the onions and garlic and fry in oil until transparent. Add the cubes of meat and brown, stirring. Add the tomatoes and bacon, and cook briefly together, adding the wine. Season with salt and pepper. Add enough water to just cover the meat. Braise gently for 2 hours on low heat. • Bring the salted water to a boil and cook macaroni about 10 minutes, until 'al dente'. • Heat the oven to 400°F. Drain the macaroni. Place the meat in a large oven dish, top with the macaroni and then the cheese. Bake until the cheese is golden.
• Serve garnished with parsley.

Fettuccine with Pork Filet

Very easy, African speciality

670 calories per serving
Preparation time: 1 hour

1 lb. 2 oz. pork filet
1 large onion
2 tbs. palm oil
3 large beefsteak tomatoes
2 cloves garlic
1 chili pepper
2 tsp. lemon juice
2 tsp. honey
1 tbs. Worcestershire sauce
1 cup hot vegetable broth
1¼ cups fettuccine
3 qts. water
1½ tsp. salt
1 cup freshly grated cheddar cheese

Wash the meat, dry and cut into 1 in. cubes. Peel and chop the onions and fry in the oil with the meat. Peel the tomatoes, cut into pieces, discarding the central stalky part, and add tomatoes to the meat. Peel and crush the garlic. Halve and wash the chili pepper, finely chop and add to the meat. • Stir in the salt, pepper, lemon juice, Worcestershire sauce, vegetable stock and stew gently for 30 minutes. • Bring the salted water to a boil, add the pasta and cook for about 8 minutes, until 'al dente'. Drain in a colander and serve topped with the meat sauce. • Sprinkle cheese over just before serving.

Wholemeal Spaghetti with Tofu Bolognese

A meal in itself, economical

690 calories per serving
Preparation time: 35 minutes

1¼ cups tofu (bean curd)
1 tbs. soy sauce
1 pinch each dried oregano, basil and black pepper
1 small green pepper
2¼ cups very ripe tomatoes
1 bouquet garni
2 onions
3 cloves garlic
6 tbs. olive oil
½ carton cream (4 oz.)
4 qts. water
2 tsp. salt
¼ cups wholemeal spaghetti
10 black olives
2 tbs. snipped chives
½ tsp. paprika powder
1 pinch cayenne pepper

Mash the tofu with a fork, and mix with the soy sauce, oregano, basil and pepper. Quarter the green pepper, wash, remove stalk, ribs, seeds, and dip with the tomatoes into boiling water. Finely shred the pepper, peel the tomatoes and dice. • Peel the onions and the garlic, finely chop and fry in the oil until transparent. Fry the tofu for 2 minutes and then add the prepared vegetables and fry for an additional 1 minute. Add the bouquet garni. Pour the cream over and cook in a covered pan for 10 minutes. • Bring the salted water to a boil, and cook the spaghetti for 8 minutes. Strain and place in a preheated serving dish. • Pit the olives, chop and stir into the sauce with the chives, paprika and cayenne. Divide the sauce over the spaghetti.

Spaghetti with Calves Kidneys

Quite expensive, very simple

620 calories per serving
Preparation time: 1 hour

14 oz. calves kidneys
1 can peeled tomatoes (14 oz.)
1 bunch parsley
1 onion
3 tbs. oil
1 pinch each salt and freshly milled white pepper
1 tsp. flour
1 tbs. butter
3 tbs. dry Marsala wine
4 qts. water
2 tsp. salt
1¾ cup spaghetti

Split the kidneys and carefully remove skin and white tubes from the inside; soak for 30 minutes, changing the cold water several times. • Drain and chop the tomatoes. Wash and dry the parsley, and finely chop. Peel the onions and slice into rings; fry in oil until transparent. Add the tomatoes, salt and pepper. Allow the sauce to thicken in an uncovered pan over medium heat. • Dry the kidneys, slice, and dust with flour. Heat the butter in a pan and brown the kidneys quickly. Blend in the Marsala wine. As soon as the wine has evaporated, mix the kidneys and parsley into the tomato sauce, seasoning again. • Bring the water to a boil, and add salt and spaghetti. Cook the spaghetti for about 8 minutes, until 'al dente', then drain in a sieve and serve immediately with the kidneys.

Pasta with Lamb Ragout

Very easy, Greek specialty

810 calories per serving
Preparation time: 1 hour

1½ lbs. shoulder of lamb
2 garlic cloves
1 sprig rosemary
3 tbs. oil
1 tbs. butter
1 tbs. tomato paste
½ cup beef broth
1 pinch each salt and freshly milled white pepper
3 qts. water
1½ tsp. salt
1¼ cups green noodles (fettuccine verdi)

Wash, dry and cut the meat into chunks, discarding all bones. Peel the garlic, wash the rosemary and chop, discarding the coarse twigs. Finely chop the garlic and rosemary needles. • Heat the oil, and brown the meat on all sides over medium heat. Pour off excess fat. Add the butter, garlic and rosemary. Stir the tomato paste into the beef broth and pour over. Season the meat with salt and pepper. Cook, covered, for 30 minutes. • Bring the water to a boil and add salt and noodles. Cook until 'al dente', about 8 minutes, then strain in a colander and place in a preheated serving dish. Top with the ragout. • A freshly-made tomato salad goes well with this.

Pasta Noodles with Rabbit Stew

Very simple

400 calories per serving
Preparation time: 1 hour

4 leaves sage
1 sprig rosemary
2 cloves garlic
3–4 tomatoes
1 oven-ready rabbit, weighing 3¼ lbs.
2 tbs. oil
1 tbs. butter
1 bay leaf
1 pinch salt
1 pinch nutmeg
½ cup white wine
2 tbs. pine nuts
1¼ cups pasta twists
3 qts. water
1½ tsp. salt

Wash and pat dry the sage and the rosemary. Peel the garlic. Skin the tomatoes and cut into chunks. Joint the rabbit into 8–10 pieces, wash, carefully discarding all splinters of bone, and dry. • In a large pan, heat together the oil and butter, toss the herbs, bay leaf and garlic briefly in the pan, then brown the joints of meat well on all sides, and season with salt and nutmeg. Pour the wine over and allow liquid to reduce to half in the uncovered pan, turning the rabbit joints. Add the tomatoes and pine nuts, and cook, covered, for 20 minutes. • Cook the twists in boiling water for approx. 8 minutes until 'al dente', then drain in a colander.
• Remove and discard the rosemary, sage and garlic from the rabbit stew before serving. • A green salad goes well with this.

Tagliatelle with Veal Ragout

Italian specialty

600 calories per serving
Preparation time: 1½ hours

1 can peeled tomatoes (14 oz.)
2 cloves garlic
1 sprig rosemary
1 lb. 2 oz. veal shoulder
2 oz. lean bacon
2 tbs. butter
½ cup dry white wine
1 pinch each salt and freshly milled white pepper
½ cup mushrooms
1¼ cup narrow ribbon noodles (either linguine or tagliatelle)
3 qts. water
1½ tsp. salt

Drain the tomatoes, retaining the juice from the can. Peel the garlic and chop finely with the rosemary. Wash the meat, dry, and make slits in it to fill with the garlic and rosemary mixture. • Finely dice the bacon and fry in 1½ tbs. butter, until the fat runs. Brown the veal well. Pour the wine over, and boil the liquid down to half, turning the meat from time to time. Add the tomatoes to the pan and crush them with a spoon. Season the meat with salt and pepper; cook for about 1 hour, gradually adding the tomato juice. • Wash the mushrooms, dry, slice vertically and fry in the remaining butter until the liquid has boiled off. • Cook the pasta until 'al dente'. Cut the meat into small cubes and add to the sauce with the mushrooms. Season the ragout and serve with the pasta.

Lamb and Apple Ragout with Pasta

Lengthy cooking time

880 calories per serving
Preparation time: 2½ hours

1½ lbs. lamb taken from leg joint
2 large onions
3–4 garlic cloves
5 tbs. olive oil
1 pinch each salt and black pepper
1 tsp. curry powder
1 cup hot beef broth
1 bay leaf
2¼ cups cooking apples
3 qts. water
1½ tsp. salt
1¼ cups pasta (twists or short macaroni)
1–2 tsp cornstarch
3 tbs. freshly chopped parsley

Cut the meat in coarse chunks. Peel and dice the onion. Peel the garlic and chop finely. Heat 4 tbs. olive oil in a large pan and brown the meat. Add the onions and garlic and fry briefly. Season the meat with the salt, pepper and the curry powder and dilute with broth. Add the bay leaf. Cook for 1½ hours over a low heat, with the lid on. • Quarter the apples, peel, core, chop coarsely and add to the meat 20 minutes before the end of the cooking time. • Bring the water to a boil, add the salt and the remaining oil. Cook the pasta until 'al dente'. • Blend the cornstarch with a little cold water and use to thicken the ragout. Sprinkle the parsley over and serve with the well drained pasta.

Green Noodles with Prawns

Somewhat expensive, quick

950 calories per serving
Preparation time: 30 minutes

10 oz. prawns
1 tbs. lemon juice
1 small onion
2 cloves garlic
2 tbs. butter
1 carton cream (8 oz.)
1 carton cream cheese (6 oz.)
2 cups freshly grated Parmesan cheese
4 qts. water
3 tsp. salt
1 tbs. oil
¾ cup green noodles
1 pinch each salt and freshly milled white pepper
1 tsp. dried tarragon

Rinse the prawns under cold water in a colander, drain and sprinkle with lemon juice. Peel and finely chop the onion. Peel and crush the garlic. • Heat the butter in a large pan, and briefly fry the prawns. Add the diced onion and garlic and fry lightly. Pour the cream and cream cheese over the prawns and bring to a boil. Add ½ cup Parmesan, and leave the prawns to cook over low heat for 5 minutes. • Bring the water to a boil, add salt, oil and pasta. Cook pasta until 'al dente', then leave to drain well. Season the creamy prawn sauce with salt, pepper and tarragon, and serve with the Parmesan to accompany the pasta.

Spaghetti with Breast of Chicken

Very simple, economical

600 calories per serving
Preparation time: 40 minutes

2 onions
1 lb. 2 oz. chicken breasts
¾ cup canned sweet corn
1 tbs. corn oil
1 cup chicken broth (instant)
1 pinch each salt and hot paprika
4 qts. water
2 tsp. salt
1 tbs. oil
1¾ cups spaghetti
3 tbs. snipped fresh chives

Peel the onions and finely dice. Wash and dry the meat, discard skin and bones, and cut evenly into small pieces.

Drain the sweet corn. • Heat the oil and fry the onion until golden. Then fry the meat cubes until golden. Stir in the corn, the chicken broth with salt and paprika, and cook gently over low heat for 15 minutes. • Bring the water to a boil, adding salt and oil. Cook spaghetti for about 8 minutes, until 'al dente'. • Place the well-drained pasta in a preheated serving dish, and spoon the chicken ragout over the spaghetti, mix together and sprinkle with chives before serving.

Tip: Try adding 3 tbs. cream to the ragout for a richer dish.

Tortellini with Chervil and Cheese Sauce

Quick, simple

570 calories per serving
Preparation time: 30 minutes

4 qts. water
2 tsp. salt
1 tbs. oil
2½ cups fresh tortellini stuffed with meat
1 onion
2 tbs. butter
1 heaping tbs. flour
½ cup hot beef broth
½ cup dry white wine
1 cup cream
1 pinch each salt and freshly milled white pepper
1 pinch freshly grated nutmeg
1 cup mozzarella cheese
½ cup chervil
1 egg yolk

Bring the water to a boil, and add oil and salt. Cook the tortellini for about 10 minutes. Peel and finely chop the onion. • Heat the butter. Fry the chopped onion, stir in the flour and fry until golden, and gradually add the stock. Bring the sauce to a boil, stirring constantly. • Add the wine and cream and heat further. Season the sauce with salt, pepper and nutmeg. Place the mozzarella cheese in the sauce in small pieces over a low heat, and allow to melt. Wash the chervil, discard coarse stems, chop roughly, and stir into the sauce. • Beat the egg yolk with 2 tbs. of sauce, and blend. • Drain the tortellini well and mix into the sauce.

Pasta with Fennel Sauce

Quick, easy

690 calories per serving
Preparation time: 30 minutes

1 bulb fennel
2 sticks celery
1 green pepper
1 cup each dry white wine and instant vegetable broth
½ carton cream (4 oz.)
1 tsp. arrowroot (or cornstarch)
1 pinch each salt and freshly milled white pepper
1 tsp. soy sauce
4 qts. water
2 tsp. salt
1¾ cup pasta of your choice, e.g. gnocchi, elbows, or rigatoni
1 tbs. freshly chopped parsley

Cut the root end and the green leaves off the bulb of fennel, retaining the green parts. Remove the hard white bits from the outside, wash the fennel bulb, and slice, then cut into narrow strips. Clean the celery sticks in a similar manner, set the tender leaves aside, wash, dry and cut into paper thin slices.
• Halve the green pepper, discarding the core, white ribs and seeds. Dice the flesh. • Bring the wine to a boil with the vegetable broth and simmer the prepared vegetables for 10 minutes.
• Blend cream with the arrowroot or cornstarch, salt, pepper and soy sauce, and thicken the sauce.
• Bring the salted water to a boil, and cook the pasta according to the instructions on the packet. Wash some of the green parts of fennel and the celery sticks, dry, finely chop and sprinkle over the prepared sauce with the parsley.

• Serve the sauce with the cooked, drained noodles.

Penne with Creamed Artichokes

Somewhat expensive, quick

570 calories per serving
Preparation time: 20 minutes

4 qts. water
2 tsp. salt
3 tbs. olive oil
1¾ cups penne (quills)
1 cup freshly cooked artichoke hearts
1 cup cream cheese
1–2 pinches freshly milled white pepper

Bring the water to a boil, and add salt and 1 teaspoon olive oil. Cook the pasta in the swiftly boiling water for about 8 minutes until 'al dente'. • Pass the artichokes through a sieve; stir the cheese in a bath of hot water until creamy and smooth. Slowly blend in the rest of the oil, and season the cream with salt and pepper. Mix in the artichoke purée. Gradually stir some of the pasta cooking water into the creamy cheese sauce.
• Drain the pasta in a sieve, and mix well with the creamy sauce in a preheated serving dish.

Home-Made Pasta with Ragout of Duck

Takes time

640 calories per serving
Preparation time: 1¾ hours

| 2¾ cups flour |
| 4 eggs |
| 1 pinch salt |
| 1 onion |
| 1 carrot |
| 1 stick celery |
| 1 bunch parsley |
| 4 sage leaves |
| 4 sprigs basil |
| 3 oz. cooked ham |
| 1¼ cups very ripe tomatoes |
| 1 small oven-ready duck |
| 3 tbs. olive oil |
| 1 cup dry red wine |
| 1 bay leaf |
| 2 cloves |
| 1 pinch each salt and freshly milled black pepper |
| 4 qts. water |
| 2 tsp. salt |
| 1 duck liver or 2 oz. chicken livers |
| 1 tsp. butter |

Using the flour, eggs and salt, prepare a pasta dough as described on page 8, and leave to rest for 1 hour. • Peel the onions, scrape the carrots, clean the sticks of celery; cut the vegetables into rings. Finely chop the herbs, and the ham. Peel the tomatoes and cut into chunks.
• Joint the duck into 8 or 10 pieces, wash and dry. Brown the vegetables, herbs, ham and duck pieces in the oil for 10 minutes, turning. Pour in the wine and evaporate. • Add the tomatoes, bay leaf, cloves, salt and pepper. Cook the duck pieces for about 50 minutes. • Roll out the pasta dough thinly on a floured board, roll up like a log roll, and cut into strips ½ in. wide. Cook the pasta in swiftly boiling water for about 4 minutes. • Cut the liver into pieces and brown in the butter, then mix into the ragout.
• Serve the noodles with the duck ragout.

Macaroni with Soy Sauce

A complete meal in itself, quick

480 calories per serving
Preparation time: 20 minutes

4 qts. water
1 tsp. salt
1 tbs. oil
1¾ cups wholewheat macaroni
1 cup bean sprouts
½ cup hot vegetable broth
4 tbs. Indonesian soy sauce
½ cup soft tofu (bean curd)
2 tbs. cream
1 pinch each salt and freshly milled white pepper
1 tbs. freshly chopped parsley

Bring the water to a boil, adding the salt and oil. Cook the macaroni, stirring thoroughly once, for about 10 min-utes, or until 'al dente'. • Drain the bean sprouts, mix the vege-table stock with the soy sauce, tofu, cream, salt and pepper to taste. • Drain the macaroni in a colander, retaining some of the cooking liquid. • Mix this liquid into the soy sauce with the bean sprouts, to make a thick sauce. • Place the macaroni in a pre-heated dish, pour the sauce over and serve garnished with chopped parsley.

Tip: You can grow bean sprouts yourself easily (see page 000). Cook the fresh sprouts in the vegetable broth for 3 minutes.

Twists with Sesame Sauce

A complete meal in itself, very easy

600 calories per serving
Preparation time: 30 minutes

4 qts. water
2 tsp. salt
1 tbs. oil
1¾ cups wholemeal pasta twists
3 cloves garlic
2 large onions
4 tbs. walnut oil
1 cup sour cream
2 pinches herb seasoning
2 tbs. freshly chopped basil
5 tbs. sesame seeds

Bring the salted water and the oil to a boil and cook the pasta, stirring once, for about 8 minutes, until 'al dente'. • Peel the cloves of garlic and onions and finely dice. Heat the oil in a large pan and fry the onions and garlic, stirring constantly, until transparent. Stir in the sour cream, season with the herb sea-soning, and heat gently, stirring constantly. • Drain the twists in a sieve. Mix the basil and sesame seeds into the sauce. • Serve the well-drained noodles on a heated serving dish with the sauce poured over.

Ratatouille with Pasta

A complete meal in itself, very easy

430 calories per serving
Preparation time: 45 minutes

1 eggplant (9 oz.)
1 cup green pepper
1¼ cup zucchini
2 large onions
3 cloves garlic
4 tbs. olive oil
2 tsp. each instant vegetable bouillon powder and mild paprika
1 pinch cayenne
1 tsp. mixed herbs
1 tbs. finely chopped basil
2¼ cups tomatoes
1¼ cups wholemeal pasta twists
10 cups water
1 tsp. salt
2 tbs. snipped chives

Peel the eggplant, wash and cube. Quarter the green peppers, clean, wash and shred lengthwise, discarding white stalky bits and seeds. Wash the zucchini and roughly chop. • Peel and finely chop the onions and garlic, and fry in a large pan of oil over low heat until transparent. Add the vegetables to the onions, sprinkle in the spices and herbs (reserve half the basil), and cook for 15 minutes. • Slit around the skins of the tomatoes, briefly dip in boiling water, and peel; coarsely chop tomatoes and add to the vegetables. Cook for an additional 5 minutes. • Boil the pasta in salted water for about 8 minutes until just firm to the bite, drain in a colander. Mix the paste, remaining basil, and the chives with the vegetables.

Wholewheat Pasta with Spicy Ragout

Complete meal in one

740 calories per serving
Preparation time: 45 minutes

1¼ cups green peppers
2 onions
3 cloves garlic
6 tbs. olive oil
2¼ cups each zucchini and tomatoes
2 tsp. powdered vegetable bouillon
1 pinch freshly milled black pepper
1¼ cups wholewheat pasta twists
10 cups water
1 tsp. salt
2 pair spicy sausages
2 tsp. Pikata (spicy seasoning found in health food shops)
2 tsp. mild paprika
3 tbs. snipped chives.

Quarter, clean, wash and finely shred the pepper. Peel and finely chop the onions and garlic; fry gently with the pepper strips over a low heat. Clean, wash, dice and add to the peppers. Wash the coarsely chopped tomatoes, discarding the stalky centers. Add the tomatoes with the instant bouillon powder and the pepper to the vegetables and cook it all together over a lower heat for 15 minutes. • Cook the pasta in boiling salted water for about 8 minutes until firm to the bite; leave to drain in a sieve. • Cut the sausages in ¼ in. slices, and mix into the vegetable ragout with the paprika and the Pikata. Leave to cook for 5 minutes longer. Serve the ragout on top of the drained twists, garnished with the chives.

Turos Csusza

Economical, lengthy cooking time

940 calories per serving
Preparation time: 45
Resting time: 1 hour

1¼ cups ricotta cheese
2¾ cups flour
4 eggs
2½ tsp. salt
4 qts. water
1 tbs. oil
6 oz. lean bacon
2 tbs. pork drippings
1 carton cream (5 oz.)
1–2 pinches freshly milled black pepper

Drain the ricotta cheese in a sieve. Sift the flour on to a board, and make a hollow in the middle. Add the eggs, ½ tsp. salt, and then gradually add 1–2 tbs. water. Knead to a firm dough, and leave to rest for 1 hour. • Thinly roll out the dough, cut into ½ in. strips and then into squares ½ in. • Bring the water to a boil, adding the salt and the rest of the oil. Cook the pasta squares in the fast boiling water for about 3 minutes, rinse with boiling water and leave to drain in a colander. • Dice the bacon and fry until crisp. Heat the pork drippings in a pan and turn the noodles in it to keep them warm. Arrange the pasta squares on a heated serving dish top, with the drained ricotta cheese broken up over it. Warm the cream in a small saucepan, but do not allow to get hot. Divide the cream over the pasta and ricotta with the pieces of bacon and the bacon fat.
• Season the noodles with the pepper.

Pasta with Viennese Liver Ragout

Austrian specialty

500 calories per serving
Preparation time: 30 minutes

14 oz. calves liver
1 large onion
2 carrots
2 tbs. oil
½ cup hot beef broth
1 tsp. cornstarch
4 tbs. red wine
1 pinch salt
½ tsp freshly milled black pepper
1 pinch dried marjoram
3 qts. water
1½ tsp. salt
1¼ cups pasta of your choice (fusilli, elbows or twists)

Cut the liver into narrow strips with a sharp knife. Peel and finely dice the onion. Scrape the carrots, wash, dry and shred into narrow strips (julienne strips). • Heat the oil and fry the onion until transparent. Add the liver and stir until it loses its pinkness. Pour in the broth, add the carrot slices and cook over a low heat for 5 minutes. • Mix the tomato purée with the cornstarch and red wine, and thicken the ragout. Season with salt, pepper and marjoram. • Bring the salted water to a boil, and cook the pasta until 'al dente'. Drain the pasta and serve in a preheated dish, with the ragout on top.

Pasta with Bacon and Capers

Economical, very easy

600 calories per serving
Preparation time: 30 minutes

7 oz. cooked lean ham
2 tbs. butter
1 tbs. flour
2 cups hot chicken broth
1 hard boiled egg
1 tbs. lemon juice
2 tbs. cream
½ bunch parsley
4 qts. water
2 tsp. salt
1 tbs. oil
¾ cup pasta of your choice (fusilli, elbows, or twists)

Dice the ham. Melt the butter in a saucepan, and fry the flour until golden. Stir and add the chicken broth gradually. Let the sauce cook gently for a few minutes, stirring occasionally. • Chop the hard-boiled egg. Chop and mix into the sauce with the lemon juice, drained capers and ham. Stir in the cream. • Rinse the parsley under the cold tap, pat dry, finely chop and stir in the sauce. • Bring the water to a boil, add salt and oil, and cook the pasta until 'al dente'. • Let the cooked noodles drain in a colander, and serve immediately with the ham sauce.

Tip: Leftover morsels from grilled chicken or turkey may be used in place of the ham.

Spätzle with Emmental Cheese

Classic recipe

670 calories per serving
Preparation time: 45 minutes

¾ cup Emmental cheese	
2 large onions	
2½–2¾ cups flour	
½ cup water	
2 eggs	
2½ tsp. salt	
4 qts. water	
4 tbs. butter	

Grate the cheese. Peel the onions and cut into thin rings. • Sift the flour into a bowl, add water, eggs and ½ tsp. salt and work quickly to a soft, but not runny, dough. Add either more water or flour as required. • Bring the water to a boil with the rest of the salt. Work small pieces of the dough back and forth on a dampened workboard, stretching and pulling, and then cut the dough into narrow strips with a long knife, and place in boiling water. The spätzle may also be pushed through a coarse sieve or through a special spätzle machine into the boiling water. They are cooked when they float to the surface. • Remove them from the surface with a slotted spoon, and leave to dry off in a sieve. Keep warm. • Melt the butter in a large pan and fry the onion rings until golden. Place the spätzle in a preheated serving dish, and pile the cheese on top. Garnish with the onion rings.

Pasta with White Cabbage

Economical, takes time to make

380 calories per serving
Preparation time: 1¾ hours

1 cup flour	
2 eggs	
1 pinch salt	
1 onion	
1 small white cabbage (about 1 lb. 2 oz.)	
3 tbs. pork drippings	
1 tbs. sugar	
½ cup hot vegetable broth	
1 pinch each salt and freshly milled black pepper	
3 qts. water	
1½ tsp. salt	
1 tbs. oil	

Work the flour, eggs, salt and, little by little, the water into a pliable dough. Leave to rest under an upturned bowl for 1 hour. • Peel the onion and cut into thin rings. Remove the outside leaves from the white cabbage and discard. Cut cabbage into four parts, wash, and finely shred, discarding the stalk. • Heat the drippings, and fry the onion rings until golden, sprinkle the sugar over, and leave to caramelize in the pan. Add the stredded cabbage, briefly fry, pour the stock over, and season with salt and pepper. Cook covered, for 30 minutes. • Thinly roll out the dough on a floured board, and cut into squares 1¾ in. and leave to dry for a few minutes. • Bring the water to a boil, add the salt and the oil, and cook the squares for about 4 minutes, then drain in a colander. Mix into the cabbage and leave in a warm place for a few minutes before serving.

Rye Spätzle with Tomato Sauce

Wholemeal recipe

620 calories per serving
Preparation time: 1¼ hours

1¾ cups each wheatmeal flour and rye flour
½ tsp. ground caraway
1 pinch each sea salt and black pepper
2 tbs. freshly grated Parmesan cheese
5 eggs
1 large onion
1 clove garlic
3 tbs. olive oil
1½ cups water
1 can tomato paste (2½ oz.)
1 tbs. wheatmeal flour
1 tsp. mixed dried herbs
¼ cup freshly grated Parmesan cheese
5 tbs. cream
1–2 pinches each sea salt and black pepper
1 pinch sugar
½–1 tsp. mild paprika
2 tbs. snipped chives
3 qts. water
1½ tsp. salt

Make a soft spätzle dough from the flour, caraway, salt, pepper, Parmesan, eggs and about 4 tbs. water and leave to rest for 30 minutes. • Peel the onion and garlic and chop finely; fry in oil until transparent. Beat the water with the tomato paste, flour and herbs, pour over the onions and cook for 5 minutes, stirring. Remove the pan from the heat, and stir in 2 tbs. Parmesan and cream. Season the sauce with spices and keep hot in a large, preheated serving dish. • Shape the spätzle on a dampened wooden board, in batches, and cook in boiling salted water for 1 minute. Scoop them out with a spoon, briefly drain, and add to the tomato sauce. • Serve garnished with the remaining Parmesan and chives.

Fettuccine with Herb Purée and Vegetables

Very simple

500 calories per serving
Preparation time: 1 hour

4 onions
1¼ cups zucchini
2 green peppers
1¼ cups mushrooms
2 beefsteak tomatoes
7 tbs. cold-pressed olive oil
1 tsp. chicken bouillon powder
1 pinch black pepper
2 sprigs tarragon
1 bunch each parsley, dill and basil
6 sage leaves
2 cloves garlic
2 tbs. flaked almonds
1 pinch each salt and freshly ground black pepper
1 tbs. lemon juice
1¼ cups fettuccine
3 qts. water
1½ tsp. salt

Peel the onions, cut in half downwards and into strips. Wash the zucchini, halve and slice. Clean and shred the peppers. Wash the mushrooms, and halve if larger. Peel and dice the tomatoes, discarding the seeds and stalky center. • Heat 4 tbs. olive oil. First, fry the onions until transparent, and then the prepared vegetables, omitting the tomatoes, and cook 5 minutes longer. • Sprinkle the instant bouillon and the pepper over, and cook, covered, for 10 minutes over low heat. • Wash and pat the herbs dry, remove coarse stems, and chop. Peel the garlic and crush through a press. Mix with the crumbled flaked almonds and the herbs. Add the salt, pepper, lemon juice and remaining oil. • Finally, stir in the tomatoes, and simmer the ragout in an open pan, to allow liquid to evaporate a little. • Cook the pasta in salted water for 8 minutes until firm to the bite, then drain. Serve with the ragout and the herb purée.

Tarhonya with Creamy Mushroom Sauce

Hungarian specialty, takes time

600 calories per serving
Drying time: 14 hours
Preparation time: 45 minutes

2 eggs	
1 pinch salt	
2 small onions	
8 tbs. sunflower oil	
½ tsp. salt	
1 tsp. mild paprika	
1¼ cups button mushrooms	
1 tbs. flour	
A few drops lemon juice	
1 pinch black pepper	
1 carton cream (6 oz.)	

To begin with, mix the eggs and salt in a bowl, add as much flour as needed to make a very firm dough. Leave the dough to dry for 2 hours, then coarsely grate and leave spread out to dry overnight. • Peel and finely chop the onions. Fry half in 5 tablespoons oil. Toss the "pasta pearls" in the oil, and cover with water, season with salt and pepper and cook for about 6 minutes; if necessary, add more water. Just before the end of the cooking time, turn the "pasta pearls" and allow to separate in the open pan. • Clean, wash and slice the mushrooms, and fry with the remaining onions in the rest of the oil, until the juices have evaporated. Add the flour and about 2 tbs. water. Flavor with the lemon juice, and a little salt and pepper. Stir in the cream and let the sauce cook for a few minutes longer. • Serve with the "pasta pearls."

Twists with Eggplant

Economical, simple

550 calories per serving
Preparation time: 1 hour

2 cloves garlic	
4 very ripe beefsteak tomatoes	
2 small eggplants	
½ cup green olives	
1 bunch basil	
2 anchovies	
1 tbs. capers	
4–5 tbs. olive oil	
½ cup hot chicken broth	
½ tsp. each salt and pepper	
1¾ cups pasta twists (or substitute spaghetti or fusilli)	
4 qts. water	
2 tsp. salt	

Peel the garlic and crush flat. Skin the tomatoes, discarding the central stalks, and chop the flesh into chunks. Wash the eggplants, dry and dice. Quarter the peppers, clean, dry, and shred finely. Pit and coarsely chop the olives. Wash and pat dry basil, and chop finely with anchovies and capers. • Heat the oil, fry the garlic until brown, then discard. Fry the diced eggplant, then add the tomatoes, the pepper strips, the anchovies, capers, olives and basil. Leave the mixture to thicken for 30 minutes, adding more broth if needed, and season with salt and pepper. • Cook the pasta until 'al dente' in boiling salted water, then drain and mix in a preheated serving dish with the vegetables.

Pasta with Bean Sprouts

Specialty from Singapore

480 calories per serving
Preparation time: 30 minutes

3 qts. water
1½ tsp. salt
1 tbs. oil
1¼ cup vermicelli
1½ cups bean sprouts
2 fresh chili peppers
2 scallions
2 tbs. fresh root ginger
10 oz. port filet
3 tbs. each sesame seed oil and soy sauce
1 pinch each salt and freshly milled white pepper

Bring the salted water and oil to a boil, and shake the vermicelli into the swiftly boiling water, stir once and cook for 4 minutes. Drain the pasta. • Rinse and drain bean sprouts in a colander. Clean, wash, dry and cut the chili peppers and scallions into rings. Peel and finely chop the ginger. Wash, dry and cut the pork filet in about ¼ in. strips.
• Heat the oil in a wok or a large saucepan, and fry the ginger, stirring constantly. Add the meat and cook together for 2 minutes. Add bean sprouts, chilies, and scallions and stir-fry for 3 minutes. • Finally, stir in the well-drained pasta and cook for 3 minutes. Season the pasta with soy sauce, salt and pepper.
• Serve with soy sauce.

Glass Noodles from Thailand

Special, somewhat expensive

600 calories per serving
Preparation time: 1 hour

1 cup "glass" noodles (transparent)
1¾ cups onions
1 small red pepper
3 cloves garlic
9 oz. pork filet
3 tbs. oil
1½ cups bean sprouts
3 tbs. soy sauce
2 tbs. oyster sauce (bought ready-made)
1 pinch salt
2–3 tbs. sugar
Juice from ½ lemon
8 oz. shrimp
2 tbs. chopped parsley or 1 tsp. chopped coriander
For frying: 3 cups oil

With scissors, cut the glass noodles into pieces of about 3 in. in length. Heat the oil to 350°F in either a frying pan or deep fryer. Deep fry the noodles in batches until golden, then lift from oil with draining spoon and leave to dry. • Peel the onions and cut into rings. Halve the red pepper, remove stalky part, ribs, seeds and white pit, and dice finely with the peeled garlic. Cut the pork filet into shreds about ½ in. thick, and fry for 2 minutes, turning constantly; remove from the oil.
• Sauté the onion rings, garlic and pepper pieces in the oil for 2 minutes. Flavor the vegetables with the sauces, the salt, the sugar and the lemon juice. Stir-fry for another 5 minutes. • Mix the pasta, the meat and the shrimp together, and heat. Garnish with parsley.

Bami Goreng

Specialty, expensive

550 calories per serving
Preparation time: 45 minutes

3 qts. water
1½ tsp. salt
1¼ cups Udon (Chinese wheatmeal pasta or substitute thin spaghetti)
10 oz. chicken breast filets
1¼ cups Chinese leaves
4 scallions
3 sticks celery
1 small red pepper
2 cloves garlic
5 tbs. oil
9 oz. shrimp
1 cup (scarce) chicken broth
2 tbs. soy sauce

Bring the salted water to a boil and cook the pasta, stirring thoroughly once, for 8 minutes, until firm to the bite.
• Wash, dry and shred the chicken breast filets in strips ½ in. thick. Drain the pasta in a colander.
• Clean the Chinese leaves, rinse in lukewarm water, dry and shred. Clean the scallions and cut into rings. Wash and dry the celery, remove coarse threads and then slice finely. Wash the pepper in warm water, dry, halve, and remove seeds, stalk and white pit, and dice. Peel and finely chop the garlic. • Heat 4 tbs. oil and fry the meat for 2 minutes, turning, then remove. Mix the shrimp and the chicken meat, the broth, and soy sauce, and season with salt. Cook covered over low heat for a few minutes. • Heat the remaining oil in another pan and warm the pasta. Mix the vegetables with the pasta.

Pea-Flour Pasta with Curry Sauce

Time consuming

830 calories per serving
Preparation time: 2 hours

1 cup Besan (chickpea flour, or substitute pea-flour from yellow peas)
1 tsp. baking powder
2 tbs. oil
8–9 tbs. water
½ tsp. salt
1 pinch cayenne pepper
4 onions
2 apples
1 lb. 2 oz. lamb shoulder
¼ cup butter
2 heaping tbs. curry powder
1 firm banana
1 carton sour cream (6 oz.)
To fry: 4 cups oil

Work the pea-flour, baking powder, oil, water, salt and cayenne pepper into a dough, and leave covered for 1 hour.
• Peel and dice the onions and apple. Cube the lamb in 1¼ in. pieces. Melt the butter in a large frying pan, and brown the meat on all sides for 2 minutes, add the onion and apple, season and cook for 5 minutes more. Mix the curry powder into the sauce and simmer, covered over low heat for 30 minutes. • Peel and slice the bananas, and mix into the sauce with sour cream. Gently cook for another 30 minutes.
• Thinly roll out the pasta dough on a floured workboard, and cut into ½ in. wide strips. • Heat the oil to 350°F and deep-fry the pasta in batches until golden. Drain and serve with curry sauce.

Japanese Noodles with Horseradish

Specialty, a bit expensive

600 calories per serving
Preparation time: 40 minutes

4 qts. water
1 tsp. salt
1¾ cups Udon (Japanese wheatmeal pasta)
3 onions
1¼ cups button mushrooms
1¼ cups carrots
4 tbs. oil
9 oz. shrimp
4 tbs. soy sauce
4 tbs. sweet and sour sauce
1 large white horseradish

Bring the salted water to a boil and cook the pasta for about 8 minutes, until firm to the bite, then drain in a colander.

• Peel and finely chop the onions. Clean the mushrooms and slice. Scrape the carrots under warm running water, dry and grate.
• Heat the oil in a large pan and fry the chopped onions. Add the mushrooms and carrots and stir-fry for 3 minutes. • Mix in the shrimp, soy sauce, sweet and sour sauce and the cooked pasta. Keep warm on very low heat. • Peel the radish, wash, dry and grate, season to taste, and offer with the pasta.

Chow Mein

Chinese specialty, a bit complicated

620 calories per serving
Preparation time: 1 hour

12 black dried mushrooms (Mu Err)
3 qts. water
1½ tsp. salt
1¼ cups Chinese egg noodles
14 oz. pork filet
1–2 tbs. cornstarch
3 tbs. soy sauce
2 scallions
2 carrots
1 cup bean sprouts
4 tbs. oil
To fry: 4 cups oil

Leave the dried mushrooms to soak covered with lukewarm water. • Bring the salted water to a boil and cook the egg noodles for 6 minutes, then shake in a colander, rinse with cold water and dry on paper towels. • Cut the pork filet into strips ½ in. thick. First dip into the cornstarch and then turn in 1 tbs. soy sauce. • Peel the onions and cut into rings. Scrape and wash the carrots, dry and cut into thin slices. • Heat the oil for frying either in a deep fryer on in a frying-pan to 350°F. Fry the pasta in portions one after the other until crispy and brown, then drain on absorbent paper, and keep warm. • Heat the oil in a pan and fry the meat, stirring, for 2 minutes. Add the carrots, the onion rings, and the rinsed, drained, bean sprouts; stir-fry altogether for 3 minutes more. • Add the mushrooms with the soaking liquid and the rest of the soy sauce to the meat, and cook together for 2 minutes. Season the ragout with salt, and thicken gradually with 1 tsp. of cornstarch, blended with some soy sauce. • Serve with the noodles.

Beef Olives with Glass Noodles

Vietnamese specialty, expensive

480 calories per serving
Preparation time: 1½ hours

14 oz. club steak
2 cloves garlic
2 tbs. cornstarch
2 tbs. each soy sauce and sherry
1 pinch each salt, white pepper and Chinese 5-spice
3 tbs. oil
1 cup glass noodles
4 scallions
4 cups water
Juice of 1 lemon
½ cup each soy sauce and sherry
16 lettuce leaves
16 slices cucumber

Remove any gristle from the club steak, and cut the meat into 16 thin slices. Peel garlic and crush through garlic press, and mix with cornstarch, soy sauce, sherry, salt, pepper, Chinese 5-spice and 2 tbs. oil. Coat the slices of meat on both sides with the mixture and leave to marinade for 1 hour. • Pour cold water over the glass noodles and leave to soften for 10 minutes. • Clean the scallions, wash and cut into thin slices. • Cover the marinated slices of meat with scallions, roll up and secure on wooden skewers. • Bring the water to a boil. Dip the pasta in for 1 minute, then drain in a colander. • Heat the remaining oil in a pan and keep the noodles warm. Place the skewered meat on a grill and cook for 5–7 minutes, turning frequently. • Mix the lemon juice with the soy sauce and sherry, and divide into 4 side bowls. • Arrange the salad leaves, cucumber slices and pasta on 4 plates, and put the skewers on top of the salad. To eat, wrap the meat, olives and pasta in salad and dip into the sauce.

Glass Noodles with Egg Sauce

Chinese specialty, quick

550 calories per serving
Preparation time: 30 minutes

8 dried black mushrooms (Mu Err)

1¼ cup glass noodles

14 oz. pork filet

4 scallions

4 tbs. oil

½ tsp. salt

⅛ well-flavored hot chicken broth

6 tbs. dry sherry

4 tbs. soy sauce

3 qts. water

4 egg yolks

Cover the mushrooms with lukewarm water, and leave to soak. Cut the glass noodles into pieces about 2½ in. long with scissors and soften in cold water for 10 minutes. • Cut the pork filet into strips ½ in. wide. Clean the scallions, wash thoroughly, dry and cut into thin rings. • Heat the oil. Stir-fry the meat for 2 minutes, and season. Add the rings of spring onions, the stock, sherry, soy sauce and mushrooms with the soaking water to the meat mixture, bring to a boil and cook for 1 minute. • Bring the water to a boil and cook the noodles swiftly for 1 minute, drain well and arrange on 4 preheated dishes. Beat the egg yolks and pour over the noodles. Divide the piping hot meat sauce over each serving of noodles.

Rice Noodles with Beef

A special dish, a bit expensive

620 calories per serving
Preparation time: 1 hour 15 minutes

1¼ cups wide rice noodles

14 oz. rump steak

2 tbs. soy sauce

2 tbs. sake (rice wine)

1 tbs. cornstarch

4 scallions

1¼ cup mushrooms

3 qts. water

5 tbs. oil

1¼ cups bean sprouts

1 tsp salt

2 tsp. sugar

3 tbs. white wine vinegar

1 pinch freshly milled black pepper

Leave the noodles to soak for 1 hour covered in cold water. • Cut the steak into strips ½ in. thick. Mix 2 tbs. soy sauce with the rice wine, and turn the strips of meat in it. Then turn in the cornstarch, cover and leave to marinate. • Wash, dry and cut the scallions into rings. • Bring the water to a boil, and cook the noodles swiftly for 1 minute, shake in a colander, rinse with cold water and drain. • Heat the oil in a wok or high-sided pan, and fry the meat strips for 2 minutes, remove, cover and keep warm. • Fry the onion rings for 1 minute in oil, add the mushrooms and the rinsed bean sprouts, and add with the rest of the salt, sugar, vinegar and pepper, and cook for 3 more minutes. • Combine the noodles and the meat. Stir-fry for 2 minutes.

Pasta Baked
and Stuffed

Pasta Roulade with Spinach-Beet

Time consuming

640 calories per serving
Preparation time: 2½ hours

1¼ cups flour
2 eggs
1 pinch salt
2 tsp. oil
Approx. ½ cup lukewarm water
2¼ cups spinach-beet
8 cups water
1 tsp. salt
2 shallots
1 clove garlic
2 tbs. butter
1 pinch white pepper
½ tsp. salt
7 oz. lean cooked ham, thinly sliced
1¼ cups ricotta
1 cup cream
1 cup mozzarella cheese
½ bunch parsley
1 pinch grated nutmeg
4 qts. water
1 tsp. salt
2¼ cups tomatoes
1 pinch each dried thyme and basil
¼ cup freshly grated Parmesan cheese
For the cooking dish: butter

Mix the flour with the eggs, salt, 1 tsp. oil and as much water as needed to form a smooth shiny dough. Shape the dough into a large sausage-shape, brush with remaining oil and leave to rest under an inverted dish for 1 hour. • Remove the root end from the spinach-beet, wash thoroughly, and remove the green parts from the stems, cut both into narrow strips and blanch in the boiling salted water for 2 minutes before draining in a colander. • Peel shallots and garlic, finely chop and mix with butter, pepper, 1 pinch of salt and the spinach-beet. • Dice the ham, and mix with the ricotta and cream. Dice the mozzarella. Chop the parsley and add to the cream mixture with half the mozzarella, nutmeg, salt and pepper. • Roll out the pasta dough into a rectangle on a floured cloth. Spread with the cream and ham mixture and the spinach-beet. Roll up the dough, using the cloth, dab the ends of the roll with water, and firmly shape into a circle. • Place the pasta roll in a very large saucepan, and cook in boiling water for about 30 minutes. • Slit the tomatoes around the bottoms, place in boiling water, peel, discard the central stalky parts and sauté with the herbs until the liquid almost vanishes. Then mix with the remaining mozzarella.

• Heat the oven to 500°F, and butter a round oven dish. Carefully place the pasta roll into the oven dish, cover with tomato sauce, sprinkle with Parmesan and bake for 15 minutes.

Tip: If no spinach-beet is available, tender young spinach may be substituted. If a sufficiently large pan is not available for cooking the pasta roll, shape two stuffed roulades from rectangles of dough, and cook these in salted water in two saucepans for about 20 minutes. The leftover roulade can be re-heated well. Cut it into thick slices, dot with butter and Parmesan, and bake in a preheated 425°F oven for 10 minutes.

Classic Cannelloni

Italian specialty

710 calories per serving
Preparation time: 1 hour
Baking time: 45 minutes

| 1 large onion |
| 2 cloves garlic |
| 9 oz. ground beef |
| 2 tbs. olive oil |
| 1 pinch each salt and freshly milled black pepper |
| ½ tsp. each dried oregano and sage |
| 2 tsp. tomato paste |
| 14 oz. canned peeled tomatoes |
| 1¼ cups cannelloni |
| 10 cups water |
| 1 tsp. salt |
| 1¼ cups grated Parmesan cheese |
| 3 tbs. sour cream |
| ¼ cup butter |

Peel and finely chop the onions and garlic, brown in oil with the ground beef for a few minutes. • Remove from heat, season with salt, pepper, crushed herbs and tomato paste, and leave to cool. • Heat the oven to 400°F. Crush the tomatoes, heat with can juice, uncovered, until some of the liquid has evaporated. • Pre-cook the cannelloni, if necessary, in boiling salted water. • Stir half the Parmesan cheese with the sour cream into the meat, and fill the tubes. Pour the tomato sauce over, sprinkle with the rest of the cheese, and top with dabs of butter. • Bake the cannelloni in the oven for 45 minutes. • A green salad goes very well with this.

Cannelloni with Vegetable Filling

Economical, easy to make

690 calories per serving
Preparation time: 45 minutes
Baking time: 20 minutes

| 1 large Spanish onion |
| 2 young carrots |
| 1 small kohlrabi |
| 2 tbs. olive oil |
| 1¼ cups frozen peas |
| 3 tbs. freshly chopped parsley |
| 1 tbs. each freshly chopped thyme and basil or |
| ½ tsp. each if dried |
| 5 tbs. dry white wine |
| 1¼ cups cannelloni |
| 10 cups water |
| 1 tsp. salt |
| 1 pinch each salt and freshly milled white pepper |
| 1 cup cream |
| 1¼ cups freshly grated Pecorino cheese |
| ¼ cup butter |

Peel and finely chop the onions, scrape, wash and shred the carrots into julienne strips. Peel and dice the kohlrabi. Heat the oil and fry the onion until transparent. Add the prepared vegetables with the peas, the herbs and wine, and sauté for 5 minutes, leave to cool. • If necessary, pre-cook the pasta in boiling salted water. • Preheat the oven to 500°F. Mix the vegetables with salt, pepper, cream and ¼ cup Pecorino and use to fill the drained cubes. • Butter a baking dish well, and lay the cannelloni in, top with the rest of the grated cheese, sprinkle with dabs of butter and bake for 20 minutes.

Kärntner Schlickkrapfen

Specialty

640 calories per serving
Preparation time: 1¾ hours

2½ cups flour
4 eggs
2 pinches salt
¾ lb. cooked meat
1 onion
1 bunch parsley
1 tbs. pork drippings
1 pinch freshly milled black pepper
1 pinch each dried thyme and marjoram
1 egg white
4-6 qts. water
2 tsp. salt

Using the flour, 3 eggs, 1 pinch salt and water as needed, make a pliable pasta dough. Leave the dough to rest for 1 hour, covered. • Put the meat through grinder or chop very finely. Peel and finely chop the onion. Wash, pat dry and chop the parsley. • Heat the drippings in a pan, and fry the onion until transparent, then add the meat. Mix with 1 pinch salt, pepper, thyme, marjoram and the parsley. Briefly cook the meat, then mix in the remaining egg. • Roll out the dough gradually on a floured workboard until 1/16 in. thick. Place the filling with 1 teaspoon on one half of dough (about 2 in. apart) and brush between the filling with lightly beaten egg white. Place the second half of the dough on top, and press down firmly between the spoonfuls of stuffing. Cut out four-cornered "ravioli" with a pastry wheel. • Bring the salted water to a boil in a large saucepan, and cook the "pockets" for about 5 minutes. • These are very good as ingredients in a meat consommé, or baked in butter with a tomato sauce.

Tyrolean Stuffed Pasta

Specialty

640 calories per serving
Preparation time: 1¾ hours

1½ cups each wheat and ryemeal flour or 2½ cups wheatmeal
3 eggs
2 pinches salt
2¼ cups spinach
½ cup butter
1 pinch white pepper
1 pinch grated nutmeg
½ cup grated Emmental
1 egg white
4 qts. water
2 tsp. salt
6 tbs. snipped chives

Using the flour, eggs, 1 pinch salt and water as needed, make a pliable pasta dough. Leave the dough to rest for 1 hour, covered. • Wash the spinach thoroughly, and cook over a moderate heat, without any added water, just the drops from rinsing, then drain, squeeze well and chop finely. • Melt 2 tbs. butter. Add the spinach, and season with 1 pinch salt, pepper and nutmeg. Let the liquid evaporate and the spinach cool. Mix in ¼ cup Emmental cheese. • Roll the dough out in 4 portions to 1/16 in. thick, and cut circles of 3½ in. diameter. With a teaspoon divide the spinach between the portions, and place on one half of each circle, painting the edges of the dough with the beaten egg white. Press the edges together into crescent-shapes, and lay on a floured cloth. • Bring the salted water to a boil, and cook the stuffed pasta for 6 minutes. Melt the rest of the butter. • Lift the stuffed pasta from the water, sprinkle with butter and serve, garnished with the snipped chives and the remaining cheese.

Stuffed Pasta Crescents

Takes a long time, Austrian specialty

790 calories per serving
Preparation time: 1¾ hours

2½ cups flour	
3 eggs	
2 pinches salt	
1 cup potatoes	
1⅓ cup ricotta	
¼ cup soft butter	
½ cup sour cream	
1 tsp. each freshly chopped mint, parsley, chervil and chives	
1 pinch black pepper	
6 oz. lean bacon	
1 egg white	
4 qts. water	
2 tsp. salt	

Using the flour, eggs, 1 pinch salt and water as needed, make a pliable pasta dough. Shape the dough into a roll, and rest for 1 hour, covered. • Peel, wash, dice and cook the potatoes in a little salted water. Mix together the ricotta, butter, sour cream and herbs, and season with salt and pepper. • Chop the bacon. Drain the potatoes well and leave to cook, then press through sieve and mix with the ricotta, etc. • Divide the pasta dough into portions and roll out into strips. • Space the spoonsful of filling evenly along the bottom half of the dough, and paint between the heaps lightly with beaten egg white. Fold the top half of the dough over, and press firmly down to seal the dough around the filling. Cut out crescent shapes. Firmly press the edges together between the thumb and forefinger. • Bring the salted water to a boil, and cook

the pasta for 5 minutes. • Crisp the diced bacon and use to garnish the well-drained pasta.

Baked Pasta Squares

Greek specialty

550 calories per serving
Drying time: 2 days
Preparation time: 35 minutes

¼ cup fine semolina
5 tbs. milk
2¼ cups flour
2 eggs
1 tsp. salt
2 cloves garlic
1 large onion
1 stick celery
2 beefsteak tomatoes
4 tbs. olive oil
1 pinch each salt, black pepper and sugar
4 qts. water
2 tsp. salt
2 tbs. chopped parsley
1 cup freshly grated Kefalotir or Parmesan cheese

Mix the semolina with the milk and leave to soak for 1 hour. • Work the flour, semolina, eggs and salt together into a firm, pliable dough. Leave the dough to rest under a hot dish for 1 hour. • Then roll the dough out in portions to the thickness of a knife, and leave the pieces to dry for 15 minutes. • Peel the garlic and onions, and dice both finely. Wash the celery, dry, discard coarse threads, and slice thinly. Peel and chop the tomatoes. • Heat the oil, and fry the onions, celery and garlic for 5 minutes, stirring. Add the pieces of tomato, season with salt, pepper and sugar, and leave to simmer, stirring from time to time. • Bring the salted water to a boil, and cook the pasta for about 5 minutes, until 'al dente', then drain in a colander. Combine with the sauce and simmer all together for 3 minutes. • Garnish the pasta and vegetable mixture with parsley and cheese before serving.

Banitza

Bulgarian specialty

740 calories per serving
Preparation time: 1 hour
Baking time: 30–40 minutes

4½ cups flour
2 pinches salt
1 tbs. wine vinegar
Approx. 1½ cups water
2 eggs
2¾ cups goats milk cheese
3 tbs. cream
1 bunch dill
1 clover garlic
1 pinch black pepper
Flour for the workboard
Oil to grease the baking tray

Mix the flour with 1 pinch salt, the vinegar and as much water as the flour absorbs, to a smooth dough, and leave to rest under a damp cloth for 1 hour. • Separate the yolks and whites of eggs to make the filling. Cream the cheese and mix with the egg yolks and cream. Wash the dill, pat dry and chop. Peel garlic, chop and crush with 1 pinch salt. Whisk the egg-whites until stiff. Stir the dill, garlic, and pepper into the cream mixture, and blend in the egg-whites gently. • Preheat the oven to 350°F. Grease a baking sheet. Shape the dough into 10 equal balls. Roll out two rolls to half the size of the baking sheet. Lay 1 piece of dough on the baking sheet, brush with oil and lay the second on top. Leave the remaining dough on one side, covered. Spread quarter of the filling on the dough, and then proceed in the same manner with the rest of the rolls and the filling. Brush the last sheets of dough with oil. • Bake the Banitza in the oven for 30 to 35 minutes, and leave to rest briefly. Cut into rectangles.

Pasta with Celery

Quick, economical

600 calories per serving
Preparation time: 40 minutes

2¼ cups celery
1 onion
1 clove garlic
2 tbs. walnut oil
½ cup each vegetable broth and dry white wine
1¾ cups pasta of your choice, e.g. twists, rigatoni or penne (quills)
4 qts. water
2 tsp. salt
3 tbs. sesame seeds
2 tsp. arrowroot (or substitute cornstarch)
3 tbs. cream
1 pinch each salt and freshly milled white pepper

Remove the coarse threads from the celery sticks and cut the ends off, retaining some tender leaves for later use. Wash the celery sticks and slice thinly. Peel and finely chop the garlic and onions. Fry until transparent in the oil. Add the celery, pour the vegetable broth and white wine over, and leave to stew for 10 minutes. • Cook the pasta in the swiftly boiling water until still firm to the bite, rinse under cold water in a colander and then leave to drain. • Toast the sesame seeds in a pan without oil until golden. • Blend the arrowroot or cornstarch with the cream until smooth, and thicken the celery juices. Let the vegetables cook for a few more minutes, season with salt and pepper and throw in the sesame seeds. • Mix the cooked pasta into the vegetables. • If desired, freshly grated Emmental cheese may be offered with this, and, to drink, the same wine used to cook the dish may be served.

Ravioli with Spinach Fillings

Italian specialty

520 calories per serving
Preparation time: 1¾ hours

2½ cups flour	
2 eggs	
1 pinch salt	
5 tbs. walnut oil	
⅓-½ cup lukewarm water	
1¼ cups spinach	
2 cloves garlic	
¼ lb. finely ground steak	
1 cup Pecorino (ewes-milk) cheese	
2 tbs. coarsely chopped pistachio nuts	
1 pinch each salt, black pepper and grated nutmeg	
3 qts. water	
1 tsp. each salt and oil	

Using the flour, eggs, 3 tbs. walnut oil and as much water as needed, make a pliable pasta dough. Coat the dough with oil and leave to rest for 1 hour, covered. • Wash the spinach thoroughly, and cook quickly for 2 minutes, in the drops of water that remain on the leaves, then press well and chop roughly. Peel and finely chop the garlic, crush and mix into the ground steak. Break up the Pecorino. Brown the steak in the remaining oil, leave to cool a little and mix with spinach, Pecorino, pistachios and spices.Roll out the dough (1/16 in. thick) in two portions on a floured workboard. Place the spinach mixture in small heaps on one piece of dough, paint around the heaps with water, lay the second piece of dough on top, and press down well between the filling to seal. Cut out with ravioli cutter, and cook, in boiling salted water to which oil has been added, for 5 minutes.

Ravioli with Cheese Filling

Takes a long time

860 calories per serving
Preparation time: 1¾ hours

6–7 eggs	
½ tsp. salt	
2 tbs. oil	
4½ cups flour	
2 cups Parmesan cheese	
2 cups ricotta cheese (italian soft-cheese)	
1 pinch white pepper	
1 pinch grated nutmeg	
8–12 cups water	
1 tsp. salt	
⅔ cup butter	

To make the pasta dough, crack 4 or 5 eggs into a bowl, according to their size. Stir in the salt and oil, add some of the flour and mix until a thin dough is formed. Sieve the rest of the flour into a bowl, add the egg mixture and work to a smooth pliable dough. Leave under an inverted dish to rest for 1 hour. • Grate the Parmesan, and mix ¾ cup with the ricotta, remaining eggs, some salt, pepper and nutmeg. • Roll out the pasta dough to 1/16 in. thick on a floured board, or process as thinly as possible in a pasta machine, then cut into 2 in. squares. Divide the filling between the squares. Wet the edges of the squares with water and firmly fold the ravioli in half. • Bring the salted water to a boil, and cook the ravioli for 5 minutes, then lift out and leave to drain. • Brown the butter slightly, stir in the remaining Parmesan and stir-fry the ravioli very carefully.

Tortellini Filled with Prawns

Takes a long time

520 calories per serving
Preparation time: 2 hours

2½ cups flour
3 eggs
1 pinch salt
¼ cup oil
10 oz. shrimp
2 tomatoes
3 shallots
3 tbs. white wine
1 tsp. cornstarch
3 tbs. sour cream
1 pinch each salt and freshly milled white pepper
1 tbs. lemon juice
2 tbs. dill
3 qts. water
1 tsp. salt
1 tsp. oil

U sing the flour, eggs, salt and 3 tbs. oil, make a workable pasta dough, and leave to rest for 1 hour, covered. • Rinse, dry and chop the shrimp. Pour boiling water over the tomatoes, peel, quarter, remove and discard seeds and stalky parts, and dice, peel the shallots and dice. Blend the cornstarch with the white wine. • Fry the shallots in the remaining oil until transparent, add the tomatoes and sour cream. Cook all together for 5 minutes, stirring. Then mix in the blended cornstarch, salt, pepper and lemon juice. • Stir the shrimp and dill into the cooled creamy sauce. • Divide the dough into portions and roll out on a lightly floured board circles of 3 in. diameter. Dampen the edges with water. Divide the filling between the circles, and fold in half pressing the edges together. • Bring the water to a boil, add salt and oil, and cook the tortellini for about 6 minutes.

Pasta Fleckerl with Veal Ragout

Takes time

710 calories per serving
Preparation time: 1¼ hours
Baking time: 10 minutes

2¼ cup flour
2 eggs
1 pinch salt
10 oz. boneless, shoulder veal
¼ lb. lean bacon
1 large onion
2 tomatoes
2 green peppers
1 tbs. pork dripping
1 tsp. mild paprika
½ cup beef broth
3 qts. water
1½ tsp. salt
3 tbs. butter
½ cup freshly grated cheese

From the flour, eggs, salt and as little water as needed, make a smooth firm dough, and leave to rest, covered, for 30 minutes. • Grind the meat. Dice the bacon, peel the onions and chop finely. Peel and chop the tomatoes. Clean the green peppers and shred. • Fry the bacon in the pork dripping, and add onions. Fry for 5 minutes together. Brown the meat, seasoning with salt and paprika. Stir in the tomatoes and strips of pepper. Pour the broth over and cook this ragout all together for 15 minutes. • Roll out the dough, but not too thinly, and cut into 2 in. squares. Leave these to dry, briefly, then cook for 4 minutes in salted water, and drain well. • Preheat the oven to 350°F. Grease a baking dish with 1 tbs. butter. • Mix the ragout with the pasta and ¼ cup cheese, place in the baking dish and dot with dabs of butter.

Bake for 10 minutes in the oven, and hand round the remaining cheese with the fleckerl.

Ham Fleckerl

Viennese speciality

830 calories per serving
Preparation time: 1½ hours
Baking time: 30 minutes

2¼ cups flour
5 eggs
2 pinches salt
7 oz. cooked lean ham
½ cup softened butter
1 pinch white pepper
1 pinch grated nutmeg
½ cup sour cream
3 qts. water
1½ tsp. salt
¼ cup white breadcrumbs
3 tbs. freshly grated cheese

Make a firm dough from the flour, 2 eggs, 1 pinch salt and some water, and leave, covered, for 30 minutes. • Dice the ham. Separate the remaining eggs. Mix ¼ cup butter with the egg yolks, and blend in the rest of the salt, pepper, nutmeg and sour cream. • Roll out the dough, but not too thinly, leave to dry, and cut into "fleckerl" 2 in. in size (squares). Cook in boiling salted water for 4 minutes, and then mix with ham into the egg mixture. • Whisk the egg-whites until stiff, and fold into the egg mixture carefully. • Preheat the oven to 400°F. Grease baking dish well with butter, and sprinkle over 2 tbs. of breadcrumbs. Fill with mixture, smoothing the top with a spoon, and sprinkle the remaining crumbs and cheese over. Drizzle the melted butter over and bake for 20 minutes.

Macaroni and Ham Pudding

Economical but lengthy cooking time

760 calories per serving
Preparation time: 30 minutes
Cooking time: 1½ hours

4 qts. water
2 tsp. salt
1 tbs. oil
1¾ cups macaroni
7 oz. smoked ham in thin slices
1 bunch chives
4 eggs
1¾ cups cream
1 large onion
Pinch salt and fresh ground white pepper
Butter for greasing the pan

Bring water and salt to a boil. Add the oil and macaroni and cook for about 10 minutes until "al dente". • Cut smoked ham into thin strips. Wash and dry chives and chop finely. • Beat the cream and the eggs and stir in with the peeled, chopped onion. Add the salt, pepper, chives and ham. • Drain the macaroni and rinse in a colander under cold water. Dry the macaroni by spreading it on cloths in a warm airy kitchen. • Boil plenty of water in a large saucepan. Line the top section of a well greased double boiler with macaroni. Cut the remaining macaroni into 1½ in. lengths. • Cover with lid or foil. Place in a double boiler saucepan which should be three-quarters full of water. • The macaroni mixture should be cooked for approximately 1½ hours on a low heat. • Check the saucepan from time to time to make sure that the water does not boil away. • Serve the pudding, turned out on to a hot dish. • Serve with a tomato sauce and fresh herbs.

Lasagne Al Forno

Specialty from Italy

870 calories per serving
Preparation time: 2 hours
Cooking time: 30–40 minutes

2 onions
2 carrots
2 bunches celery
¼ lb. lean bacon
10 oz. ground beef
¼ cup butter
½ cup red wine
1½ cups hot beef broth
1 tbs. tomato paste
Pinch of salt and fresh ground black pepper
½ cup hot milk
For the Bechamel sauce:
¼ cup butter
¼ cup flour
2 cups milk
Pinch of salt and fresh ground white pepper
Pinch of ground nutmeg
For the Lasagne sheets:
2½ cups flour
3 eggs
Pinch salt
4 qts. water
1 tsp. oil
1 tsp. salt
¾ cup mozzarella cheese
4 tbs. grated Parmesan cheese
2 tbs. butter

Peel onions, shred carrots, wash celery and dry. Chop vegetables finely and add the ground beef. Place in a bowl. • Melt the butter, add the vegetables and meat mixture and cook until lightly brown. Add salt and pepper to taste. • Pour over the wine and beef broth and simmer until liquid is absorbed. Mix the remaining liquid with the tomato paste. Add salt and pepper to taste. Stir in the milk and simmer at very low heat for approximately 1½ hours, stirring occasionally. • Meanwhile make the Bechamel sauce. Melt butter in a saucepan, add the flour and cook for 1 minute, without browning. Gradually add the strained milk, stirring constantly. Bring to a boil and simmer for 2 minutes. Season with salt and pepper to taste. • Put eggs and salt into center of flour in a bowl and mix by hand to a stiff, firm dough. Add cold water as needed. Cover the dough with a wet paper towel and leave for 1 hour. • Divide dough into portions and roll out each piece as thinly as possible on a lightly floured board or table top. • Roll up loosely and cut into strips, about 6 × 3 in. wide, with a sharp knife. • Bring water, salt and oil to a boil. Slowly drop in the lasagne and boil for about 4 minutes. • Spread the lasagne on cloths. • Dice the mozzarella. •

Preheat the oven to 350°F. • Butter a large ovenproof dish and spoon in enough sauce to cover the base. Arrange the lasagne sheets on top of the sauce. • Mix some mozzarella and Parmesan cheese between the layers. Repeat the layers until all the sauce, lasagne, cheese and Bechamel sauce are used. • Spoon over the remaining Bechamel sauce and sprinkle with cheese and a few butter knobs. • Bake in preheated over for 30–40 minutes until golden brown.

Lasagne with Spinach

Another Italian specialty

620 calories per serving
Preparation time: 45 minutes
Cooking time: 30 minutes

3 cups spinach	
2 cups water	
½ tsp. of salt	
1 cup milk	
¼ cup butter	
Pinch ground nutmeg and white pepper	
1 cup Ricotta cheese	
1 cup Pecorino cheese	
½ cup flour	
2 large tomatoes	
1¼ cups lasagne	
10 cups water	
1 tsp. of salt	
1 tbs. olive oil	
½ tsp. dried oregano	
Olive oil for greasing	

Olive oil for greasing

Wash the spinach thoroughly and put into boiling water for 2 minutes. Drain well and keep the liquid. • Melt the butter and stir in the flour, milk and liquid until light yellow. Add the nutmeg and pepper to the Bechamel sauce to taste. Mix in the Ricotta cheese. Chop the Pecorino into small pieces. Wash, dry and slice the tomatoes. • Cook the lasagne until "al dente," and drain thoroughly. • Preheat the oven to 400°F. • Line the base of a large buttered ovenproof dish with lasagne. Spoon over some spinach, top with tomatoes and sprinkle with oregano and Pecorino. • Pour over the Bechamel sauce. • Repeat the layers finishing with lasagne and Bechamel sauce and bake on the middle shelf of a hot oven for 30 minutes.

Lasagne with Savoy Cabbage

Easy to prepare

880 calories per serving
Preparation time: 1 hour
Cooking time: 40 minutes

2¼ cups savoy cabbage	
1 tsp. salt	
1 onion	
1 clove garlic	
3 tbs. oil	
14 oz. ground beef	
½ tsp. dried thyme	
Pinch black pepper	
1¼ cups lasagne	
10 cups water	
1 tsp. of salt	
3 tbs. butter and flour	
1 cup milk	
1 cup ricotta with herbs	
4 large tomatoes	
½ cup Pecorino cheese	

Butter for greasing

Chop the cabbage and cook in a saucepan of boiling salted water for 2 minutes. Drain and keep 1 cup of the liquid. • Peel onion and garlic, chop finely and fry in 2 tbs. oil together with the thyme, salt and pepper. • Boil lasagne in salted water for approximately 5 minutes. Drain well. • Melt the butter in a saucepan, add flour, cooking liquid and milk and bring to a boil. Stir in the ricotta. • Mix the cabbage, sliced tomatoes and Pecorino with half the sauce. • Transfer a little bit of sauce to a buttered ovenproof dish and repeat layers of lasagne, cabbage, ground beef, tomatoes and cheese. • Spoon over the remaining sauce. • Place the lasagne into the hot oven and bake on 400°F for 40 minutes.

Wholewheat Lasagne

Wholemeal recipe

780 calories per serving
Preparation time: 2 hours
Cooking time: 30 minutes

1¼ cup wholewheat flour
1½ tsp. sea salt
2 eggs
2 tbs. sunflower oil
2¼ cups leeks
½ cup mushrooms
½ cup olive oil
14 oz. ground beef
¼ cup wheat-corn
½ tsp. black pepper
1 cup water
1 cup cream
2 tsp. paprika powder
4 tbs. chopped parsley
2 cup grated Emmentaler cheese
¼ cup grated Parmesan
2¼ cup large tomatoes
3 tbs. butter

Measure flour, oil, salt and eggs into a bowl and make a firm dough. • Trim, clean and slice the leeks finely. Wash mushrooms, slice into fine slices and turn into hot olive oil for 5 minutes until brown. • Stir in ground beef and wheat-corn. Add salt and pepper and simmer on low heat for approximately 5 minutes. • Pour in the cream, paprika powder and parsley and allow the sauce to thicken. Grate the cheese. Slice tomatoes. Roll out the dough as thinly as possible and cut into rectangles. Boil the lasagne in salted water for 4 minutes. Drain well. • Place the lasagne into the base of a well greased ovenproof casserole dish and arrange the tomatoes, cheese and noodles in layers on top. Dot knobs of butter over top layer. • Bake in a preheated oven on 400°F for 30 minutes until golden brown.

Jollini Casserole

Easy to prepare, economical

640 calories per serving
Preparation time: 20 minutes
Cooking time: 30 minutes

3 qts. water
1½ tsp. salt
1 tsp. oil
2¼ cup jollini (pasta twists)
2¼ cups frozen peas
1 cup zucchini
¼ lb. salami cut into thin slices
¼ cup chives
1 cup sour cream
2 eggs
½ tsp. salt
¼ cup grated fontina cheese
2 tbs butter

Place the pasta twists into boiling, salted water and cook for approximately 5 minutes until "al dente." • Boil the peas in ¼ cup of salted water for 5 minutes. • Trim, clean and dice the zucchini. • Preheat the oven to 400°F. • Drain the pasta. Cut the salami in small pieces. • Place the pasta, salami, peas, zucchini and chives into a well buttered ovenproof dish. • In a bowl, beat the eggs well, then beat in the cream and salt and pour over the pasta mixture. • Sprinkle the cheese over the top. • Bake on middle shelf of hot oven for 30 minutes until golden brown.

Pasta Casserole

Economical, easy to prepare

810 calories per serving
Preparation time: 30 minutes
Cooking time: 40 minutes

3 qts. water
1 small onion
¼ cup pasta (e.g. rigatoni or pasta quills)
10 oz. cups cooked ham
2 cups milk
2 eggs
½ tsp. cornstarch
Pinch fresh ground nutmeg
¼ cup breadcrumbs
¼ cup fresh grated Emmental cheese
2 tbs. butter
For the dish: butter for greasing

Bring a large saucepan full of salted water to a boil. • Add the pasta and peeled onion and cook until "al dente." Dice the ham. • Beat the eggs well, then beat in the nutmeg, salt, milk and cornstarch. • Drain the pasta thoroughly and mix with the diced ham in a well buttered ovenproof dish. • Pour over the beaten egg. • Sprinkle the Emmental cheese and breadcrumbs over the top. • Place on middle shelf of cold oven and bake for approximately 40 minutes on 450°F until golden brown.

Pasta Casserole with Salami

Economical, easy to prepare

640 calories per serving
Preparation time: 20 minutes
Cooking time: 30 minutes

1¾ cup spaghetti
4 qts. water
2 tsp. salt
1 small can peeled tomatoes
1 tsp. dried oregano
Pinch fresh ground white pepper
2 onions
1 clove garlic
2 oz. salami, cut in thin slices
1¾ cups sour cream
1 tbs. olive oil
3 tbs. fresh grated Parmesan cheese
2 tbs. breadcrumbs
For the dish: olive oil for greasing

Cook the spaghetti in boiling, salted water for 8 minutes until "al dente." • Mash the tomatoes. Add oregano, salt and pepper to taste. • Peel onion and cut into rings. Peel garlic clove and chop finely. • Preheat the oven to 400°F. • Place the spaghetti and tomato paste into an ovenproof dish greased with olive oil. • Put the onion rings on top. Add the salami slices. • Mix the sour cream, garlic and oil and pour over the salami slices. • Sprinkle the cheese and breadcrumbs over the top. • Bake on middle shelf of hot oven for approximately 30 minutes until crispy. • Serve with a mixed salad and fresh herbs.

Pasta with Swiss Cheese

Easy to prepare

1000 calories per serving
Preparation time: 25 minutes
Cooking time: 30 minutes

4 qts. water
1¾ cups pasta (tagliatelle or macaroni)
2 tbs. salt
1 tbs. oil
1¾ cups Gruyere cheese or Emmental
1 cup cream
Pinch of salt and fresh ground nutmeg
1 egg yolk
2 tbs. butter
2 tbs. chopped parsley

Drop the pasta into boiling, salted water and cook "al dente." Drain well. • Grate the cheese. • Whisk the cream, salt and nutmeg until stiff. • Place half the pasta into a buttered ovenproof dish. Add the cheese and finish with the remaining pasta. Pour cream over the top. • Put the dish into a cold oven and bake on middle shelf for 30 minutes on 400°F. • Sprinkle with parsley before serving. • Serve with a fresh green salad.

Noodle Nests with Beansprouts

Wholemeal recipe

670 calories per serving
Preparation time: 30 minutes

1 cup wholewheat soup noodles
2 qts. water
1 tsp. salt
¾ cup beansprouts
6 eggs
½ tsp. dried basil
½ tsp. dried thyme
Pinch curry powder
2 tbs. soy sauce
8 small lettuce leaves
¼ cup butter
1 cup Emmental cheese in 4 slices
2 oz. raw ham, cut in 8 small slices
8 small basil leaves

Place the pasta into boiling, salted water and cook for 5 minutes. • Put in a colander, hold under cold running water. Drain well. • Rinse the beansprouts under running water and drain. • Boil 4 eggs for 5 minutes and cut into halves. • Mix noodles, curry and soy sauce and the remaining eggs together. • Wash and dry lettuce leaves and place on 4 serving plates. • Melt butter and place 8 small portions of the pasta mixture into a saucepan. • Make a small hollow in the center of the pasta and place the diagonally cut ham and cheese slices into the nests. Place the egg halves on top and fold the ham and cheese slices over. • Fry the pasta for approximately 10 minutes on a low heat. • Serve on top of lettuce leaves, garnished with basil.

Pasta Casserole with Mushrooms

Expensive but easy to prepare

620 calories per serving
Preparation time: 30 minutes
Cooking time: 40 minutes

1¼ cups pasta spirals
2½ qts. water
1 tsp. salt
1¼ cups broccoli
1¼ cups mushrooms
1 clove garlic
2 tbs. oil
2 eggs
2 cups milk
Pinch salt, paprika powder and ground nutmeg
1 cup grated Parmesan cheese
1 tbs. almond flakes
1 tbs. sesame seeds
1 tbs. melted butter
For the dish: butter for greasing

Cook the pasta in boiling, salted water until "al dente." • Trim, clean and slice the broccoli and mushrooms. Peel the garlic and fry in oil. Add the broccoli and simmer for 3 minutes. • Heat the remaining oil and fry the mushrooms until golden brown. Drain the pasta. • Preheat the oven to 450°F. • Place the pasta spirals, broccoli and mushrooms into a well buttered ovenproof dish. • Separate egg whites and egg yolks. • In a bowl, beat the egg yolks well, then beat in the milk, salt, paprika, nutmeg and the Parmesan cheese. • Whisk the egg whites until firm peaks form, but not until totally stiff. Mix with the egg yolks and pour over the top. • Sprinkle the almond flakes and sesame seed on top. • Bake for 40 minutes.

Macaroni Casserole with Eggplant

Lengthy cooking time

830 calories per serving
Preparation time: 1 hour
Cooking time: 30 minutes

3 eggplants
1 tbs. salt
1¾ cups macaroni
4 qts. water
1 bunch scallions
2 carrots
¾ cup celery
1 sprig thyme
½ cup olive oil
1 large can peeled tomatoes
½ cup grated Pecorino cheese
¾ cup mozzarella cheese

Cut the eggplant in ½ in. strips. Lightly salt and leave for 20 minutes. • Break the pasta in half and cook in boiling, salted water until "al dente." • Trim, clean and finely chop the onions, carrots and celery. • Fry the chopped thyme leaves and the vegetables in 2 tbs. of oil. Add the tomatoes and simmer for approximately 10 minutes. • Preheat the oven to 425°F. • Rinse and dry the eggplant and fry in the remaining oil until brown. • Place half of the macaroni in a buttered ovenproof dish. Spread 2 tbs. of grated cheese on top. Pour over the tomato sauce. Add the eggplant and remaining noodles in layers on top. • Finish with the mozzarella cheese slices and bake for 30 minutes.

Wholewheat Pasta with Fennel

Wholemeal recipe, economical

830 calories per serving
Preparation time: 25 minutes
Cooking time: 30 minutes

2¼ cups fennel
1¼ cups wholewheat pasta shells
2½ qts. water
1 tsp. salt
4 eggs
1 cup cream
2 tbs. wheatcorn wholemeal flour
6 tbs. tomato paste
Pinch Pikata (herbs mixture) and white pepper
2 tsp. sea salt
¼ cup fresh chopped parsley
¼ cup butter
1 cup gouda cheese cut in slices

Wash the fennel in cold water, dry thoroughly and cut into thin strips. • Save feathery leaves from the fennel for the garnish. • Cook the pasta and fennel together in boiling, salted water for approximately 8 minutes until tender. • Hold under cold running water and drain well. • In a bowl, beat the eggs well, then beat in the cream, flour, tomato paste, herbs and 2 tsp. chopped parsley. • Preheat the oven to 350°F. • Place the pasta and fennel into a ovenproof dish. • Pour over the egg mixture and bake for 20 minutes. • Place the cheese slices and a few knobs of butter on top and bake for another 10 minutes. • Sprinkle with remaining parsley and fennel leaves before serving.

Tagliatelle Pie with Tomatoes

Easy to prepare, economical

790 calories per serving
Preparation time: 30 minutes
Cooking time: 20–30 minutes

1¼ cups tagliatelle
2½ qts. water
1 tsp. salt
1 fennel
3 large tomatoes
1 bunch mixed herbs, e.g. chervil, sage, dill
3 tbs. butter
½ cup cream
¼ lb. cooked ham
1¼ cups cream
½ cup milk
2 eggs
Pinch salt and freshly ground white pepper
2 tbs. breadcrumbs

Cook the pasta in boiling, salted water until tender. • Wash the fennel in cold water, dry thoroughly and cut into thin strips. • Trim feathery leaves from the fennel and save for garnish. • Slice the tomatoes. Wash and dry the herbs. • Fry the fennel in 1 tbs. butter. Add the cream, herbs and diced ham. • Preheat the oven to 400°F. • Butter an ovenproof dish. Place the pasta, fennel and tomatoes in layers into the dish. • Beat the eggs well, then beat in the cream, milk and salt and pepper to taste, and pour over the top. • Sprinkle with breadcrumbs and a few knobs of butter and bake for approximately 20–30 minutes.

Pasta Soufflé with Smoked Salmon

Expensive to prepare

740 calories per serving
Preparation time: 30 minutes
Cooking time: 30 minutes

1¼ cups small pasta shapes (e.g. pasta bow ties)
2½ qts. water
1 tsp. salt
6 eggs
1 cup cream
½ cup milk
Pinch of salt and freshly ground white pepper
¾ cup Gruyere cheese
½ tsp. paprika powder
6 oz. smoked salmon
1 bunch chives
For the dish: butter for greasing

Cook the pasta in boiling, salted water for approximately 6 minutes. • Hold under cold running water and drain well. • Separate the egg yolks from the egg whites. • Mix the egg yolks, then beat in the cream, milk, salt and pepper to taste. • Whisk egg whites until firm peaks form. Take half of the cheese and paprika powder and beat into the stiff egg white. • Dice the salmon. Wash, dry and finely chop the chives. • Mix the pasta, salmon and chives together. Add salt and pepper to taste. • Preheat the oven to 350°F. • Butter four small ovenproof dishes. Place the pasta into the dishes and pour over the egg mixture. • Sprinkle with the remaining cheese. • Place the dishes on the middle shelf of a hot oven and bake for approximately 30 minutes until golden brown. • Serve with white wine sauce or tomato salad with basil.

Macaroni Timbale

Wholemeal recipe

930 calories per serving
Preparation time: 50 minutes
Cooking time: 40 minutes

1 cup wholewheat flour
2 tbs. soya flour
½ tsp. salt
1 egg
½ cup butter
4½ cups tomatoes
3 cloves garlic
¼ cup olive oil
2 tsp. fresh chopped marjoram and basil
Pinch of black pepper
1 cup wholewheat macaroni
2 qts. water
1 tsp. salt
⅓ cup black olives
¾ cup Pecorino cheese
1 tbs. butter

Put eggs, butter and salt into center of flour in a bowl and mix by hand to a stiff, firm dough. Cover and put in a cool place. • Skin and dice the tomatoes. Peel the garlic clove and fry in oil until transparent. • Add the herbs, tomatoes and pepper. Cook for 15 minutes, until liquid evaporates. • Break the macaroni into pieces and boil in salted water for approximately 8 minutes; drain in a colander. • Take pits out of the olives and cut into small pieces. • Grate the cheese. Mix the pasta, olives, cheese and the tomato mixture. • Butter an ovenproof dish. • Roll out the dough as thin as possible. Cut out a circle the size of the top of the dish. • Place the pasta into the dish, add the filling. • Place the pastry cover on top and press firmly around the edges. Pierce a few holes into the top. • Glaze with butter. •

Bake for 40 minutes until golden brown.

Pasta Pizza

Wholemeal recipe, easy to prepare

700 calories per serving
Preparation time: 40 minutes
Cooking time: 30 minutes

2¼ cups spaghetti
5 qts. water
2 tsp. salt
2 green peppers
7 oz. salami, thinly sliced
2¼ cups tomatoes
8 eggs
1½ cups milk
1 tbs. cornstarch
1 cup grated Parmesan cheese
2 tbs. Italian herbs, paprika powder and chopped basil
1 tsp. salt
1¼ cups Emmental cheese
¼ cup olive oil
2 tbs. chives

Cook the pasta in boiling, salted water for 6 minutes. Clean and chop the green peppers. Add to the pasta and cook for another 2 minutes. Drain in a colander, hold under cold running water and dry. • Butter two ovenproof dishes. • Preheat the oven to 350°F. • Put the pasta and green peppers in the ovenproof dishes. • Place salami slices on top. • Wash and slice tomatoes and place on top of the salami. • Mix the eggs, milk, cornstarch, Parmesan and herbs and pour over the tomatoes. • Grate the Emmental cheese and sprinkle on top. • Pour over the oil. • Bake the pizza for approximately 30 minutes. • Sprinkle with chives before serving.

Macaroni Casserole

Lengthy cooking time

940 calories per serving
Preparation time: 1 hour
Cooking time: 40–45 minutes

1¼ lbs. veal escalopes
1 tbs. butter
¼ cup oil
2 bay leaves
½ cup dry white wine
1 cup cream
5 eggs
Pinch salt and fresh ground white pepper
1 tsp. dried tarragon
¾ cup macaroni
4 qts. water
2 tsp. salt
¾ cup Emmentaler cheese
1 bunch parsley
1 onion
1 cup cream

Dice the veal escalopes and fry in 2 tbs. oil. Add the bay leaves and the wine. Cover the meat and cook for 30 minutes. Leave to cool and then chop. Add cream and 1 egg to the chopped meat. Add salt, pepper and tarragon to taste. • Cook the macaroni in boiling, salted water for 8 minutes. Drain well. Pour over the remaining oil. Grate the cheese. • Preheat the oven to 400°F. • Place half of the macaroni into a buttered dish, add the chopped meat and sprinkle the parsley on top. • Peel and dice the onion. Place with half of the cheese on top of the chopped meat together with the remaining macaroni. • Mix the remaining eggs with the cream. Add the salt and pepper to taste and pour over the macaroni. • Bake for 30 minutes. • Sprinkle remaining cheese on top and bake for another 10–15 minutes until golden brown and crispy.

Wholewheat Macaroni with Spinach

790 calories per serving
Preparation time: 45 minutes
Cooking time: 35 minutes

10¼ cups wholewheat macaroni
2½ qts. water
1 tsp. salt
1 tsp. oil
5¼ cups spinach
1 onion
2 clove garlic
¼ cup butter
¼ cup wholewheat flour
½ cup hot vegetable broth
1 cup cream
¾ cup gouda cheese
Pinch white pepper

Cook the pasta in boiling, salted water until "al dente." Drain well. • Clean and wash the spinach and cook in boiling salted water for 2 minutes. • Peel and chop the onion and garlic. Fry in butter until transparent. • Add the flour and fry until light yellow. Pour in a broth and cream and bring to the boil, stirring constantly. • Shred the cheese and stir into the sauce. Season with salt and pepper to taste. • Preheat the oven to 400°F. • Place half of the macaroni into a buttered dish. Add the spinach and a third of the cheese sauce. • Place the remaining pasta and cheese sauce on top. • Bake for 35 minutes.

Russian Casserole

1100 calories per serving
Preparation time: 35 minutes
Cooking time: 40 minutes

2½ qts. water
10¼ cups tagliatelle
1 tsp. salt
3 tbs. oil
7 oz. lean bacon
2 onions
½ tsp. dried marjoram
1¾ cups ricotta
2 eggs
½ cup cream
Pinch fresh ground white pepper
⅓ cup butter
¼ cup breadcrumbs
2 tbs. chopped parsley

Cook the pasta in boiling, salted water until "al dente." Drain in a colander. • Cut the bacon in small pieces. Peel and chop the onions. Fry the bacon and onions until transparent. Stir in the pasta and marjoram. • In a bowl, whisk the ricotta and eggs. Season with salt and pepper to taste. • Preheat the oven to 350°F. • Place three-quarters of the pasta into an ovenproof dish. • Add half of the ricotta mixture and finish layering with the remaining pasta. • Sprinkle the breadcrumbs on top of the noodles. • Bake on the middle shelf of the oven for 30 minutes. • Place dish on top shelf and bake for another 10 minutes on 500°F until crispy. • Sprinkle with parsley before serving.

Turkish Pasta Pie

Economical

640 calories per serving
Preparation time: 35 minutes
Cooking time: 30 minutes

3 qts. water
1 tsp. salt
1¼ cups macaroni
¼ cup butter
3 tbs. flour
2¼ cups milk
3 eggs
Pinch freshly ground white pepper
¼ cup chopped walnuts
¼ cup freshly chopped Pecorino cheese
For the dish: butter for greasing

Cook the macaroni in boiling, salted water until "al dente." Drain in a colander, hold under cold running water. • Melt the butter in a saucepan. Add the flour and fry until light yellow. Pour in the milk and stir constantly. Simmer for 10 minutes. Leave to cool. • Preheat the oven to 400°F. • Beat the eggs well, then beat in the pepper. • Pour the sauce into a buttered ovenproof dish and place the pasta on top. • Sprinkle with walnuts. • Pour over remaining sauce and cheese. • Bake for 30 minutes until golden brown. • Serve with tomato salad and onion rings or black olives.

Macaroni Casserole with Onions

Economical, lengthy cooking time

640 calories per serving
Preparation time: 1 hour
Cooking time: 30 minutes

2½ qts. water
1 tsp. salt
1¼ cups macaroni
2¼ cups large onions
1 clove garlic
3 tbs. oil with herbs
½ tsp. salt
Pinch freshly ground black pepper
4 eggs
1 cup freshly grated Emmental cheese
2 tsp. paprika powder
1 cup sour cream
2 tbs. chopped parsley
For the dish: butter for greasing

Drop the macaroni in boiling, salted water and cook for 10 minutes until tender. Drain in a colander, hold under running cold water. • Peel and chop the onions and garlic. • Heat the oil and fry onions and garlic until transparent. Season with salt and pepper to taste. • In a bowl, whisk the eggs, sour cream, parsley, grated cheese and paprika powder. • Preheat the oven to 400°F. • Place half of the onions into a buttered ovenproof dish. Add the macaroni and put the remaining onions on top. • Pour over the creamy cheese mixture. • Place in the oven and bake for 30 minutes until golden brown and crispy.

Macaroni Casserole with Ground Beef

Specialty from Greece, lengthy cooking time

690 calories per serving
Preparation time: 1½ hours
Cooking time: 40 minutes

2½ qts. water
1 tsp. oil
1 tsp. salt
10¼ cups macaroni
2 tbs. butter
1 egg white
6 tbs. freshly grated Greek or Parmesan cheese
1 large onion
4 large tomatoes
1 lb. 2 oz. ground beef
1 tsp. salt
Pinch freshly ground white pepper and cinnamon
½ cup beef broth
2 tbs. freshly chopped parsley
½ cup dry white wine
2 tbs. flour
1½ cups milk
1 tsp. salt
4 tbs. breadcrumbs
2 tbs. butter

Cook the macaroni in salted water for approximately 8 minutes until "al dente." Hold under cold running water and drain. • Melt 1 tbs. butter in a saucepan and fry macaroni for 2 minutes. • Whisk the egg white until firm peaks form, then fold in the macaroni and 2 tbs. cheese. • Place half of the macaroni in a well buttered ovenproof dish. • Peel and chop the onion and fry in butter until transparent. • Cut the tomatoes crosswise and pour boiling water over. Leave in cold water for a few minutes. Rinse, peel and dry. • Mix the ground beef, onion, salt, pepper and cinnamon, and fry in a saucepan until meat is brown. • Stir in the tomatoes and beef broth and simmer for approximately 15 minutes. Pour in the wine and parsley. • Preheat the oven to 400°F. • Place the meat mixture on top of the macaroni and continue to layer with the remaining pasta. • Mix flour with 2 tbs. of water. Bring milk to a boil. Stir in the flour and liquid and simmer for a few minutes. • Add salt and grated cheese to taste. Pour over the sauce. • Sprinkle the breadcrumbs and butter on top. • Bake the casserole on the middle shelf for approximately 40 minutes. • Serve with a green salad.

Macaroni Casserole in an Earthenware Dish

Specialty from Greece

570 calories per serving
Preparation time: 1¼ hours
Cooking time: 45 minutes

3 onions
2 large cloves garlic
1 leek
1 celery
1 carrot
1 bunch parsley
¼ cup butter
1 lb. 2 oz. ground lamb or veal
½ tsp. salt and freshly ground black pepper
½ cup dry red wine
1 cup hot beef broth
3 qts. water
1 tsp. salt
1¼ cups macaroni
2¼ cups tomatoes
½ cup Greek or Parmesan cheese

Peel and chop the onions and garlic. • Trim, wash, dry and dice the leek and celery. • Wash, peel and dice the carrot. • Wash, dry and chop the parsley. • Melt half of the butter in a saucepan. Add the onions and fry until transparent. Stir in the garlic, leek, celery and onions. • Add the ground meat and fry until brown. • Stir in the parsley, salt, pepper and red wine. Simmer in uncovered saucepan until liquid evaporates. • Add the beef broth and simmer for another 30 minutes. • Cook the macaroni in boiling, salted water for approximately 8 minutes until "al dente." Drain well. • Place the earthenware dish in cold water. •

Cut the tomatoes crosswise. Dip in boiling water. Peel and chop. • Place half of the macaroni into the earthenware dish. Add the ground meat sauce. Put the remaining macaroni on top. Season with salt and pepper to taste and add the tomatoes. • Cover the earthenware dish and put into a cold oven and then bake for 30 minutes on 450°F. • Grate the cheese and sprinkle on top. Add a few knobs butter and bake uncovered for an additional 15 minutes until golden brown and crispy. • Vegetarians should use zucchini instead of ground meat.

Neapolitan Macaroni Casserole

Specialty from Italy

640 calories per serving
Preparation time: 1¼ hours
Cooking time: 20–30 minutes

2 eggplants	
2 tsp. salt	
2¼ cups tomatoes	
1 onion	
1 carrot	
1 celery	
½ bunch basil	
6 tbs. olive oil	
Pinch of black pepper	
1¼ cups macaroni	
2½ qts. water	
1 tsp. salt	
1 cup Pecorino cheese	
1¾ cups mozzarella cheese	
For the dish: butter for greasing	

Wash, dry and slice eggplants. Sprinkle with salt and leave for 30 minutes. • Peel and cut the tomatoes in pieces. • Peel the onion. Grate the carrot. • Trim, clean and chop the celery. • Fry all the vegetables in a saucepan except the tomatoes and eggplant. • Add the tomatoes and season with salt and pepper to taste. • Simmer until thickened. • Rinse and dry the eggplant. Heat the remaining oil and fry the eggplant until brown. • Break the macaroni into pieces and drop into boiling, salted water. Cook until tender. • Preheat the oven to 450°F. • Place the macaroni with half of the sauce into a well buttered ovenproof dish. Add the grated cheese. • Cover with eggplant. Place the mozzarella on top. • Finish with the remaining pasta, eggplant and mozzarella slices. • Pour over the remaining sauce and bake for 20–30 minutes.

Great Pasta Salads

Pasta Salad with Cheese, Tomatoes and Watercress

Easy to prepare

450 calories per serving
Preparation time: 30 minutes
Cooling time: 1–2 hours

1 cup rigatoni
2 qts. water
1 tsp. salt
1 tsp. oil
3 tbs. vinegar
Pinch of ground white pepper
2 eggs
2 bunches radish
1 small box watercress
½ bunch parsley
4 tomatoes
1 cup Emmental cheese
1¾ cups sour cream

Drop the rigatoni into boiling, salted water and cook for approximately 8 minutes until "al dente." Rinse and drain. Season with vinegar, salt and pepper to taste. • Boil the eggs for 10 minutes. Hold under cold running water, peel and slice. • Trim, wash and slice the radishes • Hold the watercress and parsley under running water, drain and chop finely. • Wash, seed and chop the tomatoes into eighths. Dice the cheese. • In a bowl, mix together the radish, herbs, cheese, sour cream and pasta. Add the tomatoes and eggs. • Put the salad in the refrigerator for 1–2 hours. • Leave at room temperature for 10 minutes before serving.

Multicolored Pasta Salad

Easy to prepare

790 calories per serving
Preparation time: 40 minutes

2½ qts. water
1¼ cups pasta of 3 different colors (e.g. white quocchi; green jollini; cranery shells)
1 tsp. salt
1 tsp. oil
2 cups low-fat yogurt
3 tbs. lemon juice
2 tsp. sugar
Pinch salt
1 cup cream
1¾ cups Emmental cheese
⅓ cup walnuts
1¼ cups blue grapes
1 pear
1 red skinned apple
½ endive

Drop the pasta into boiling, salted water for 6–8 minutes and cook until "al dente." Rinse and drain. • In a bowl, mix together the yogurt, lemon juice, sugar and salt. • Beat the cream until stiff and stir into the yogurt mixture. • Remove the rind from the cheese and cut into thin strips. Chop the walnuts. • Wash and pit the grapes and halve. Slice the apple and pear and cut into eighths. • In a bowl, mix together the nuts, cheese, pasta, fruits and yogurt mixture. • Trim, clean and wash the endive and dry thoroughly. • Separate the endive into leaves, tear into pieces and arrange onto 4 serving dishes and serve pasta salad on these.

Pasta and Parma Ham Salad

An Italian favorite

520 calories per serving
Preparation time: 30 minutes

| 1¾ cups spaghetti |
| 4 qts. water |
| 2 tsp. salt |
| ¼ cup good olive oil |
| 6 oz. parma ham |
| 10 black olives |
| 1¼ cups gorgonzola cheese |
| 1 bunch basil |
| 3-4 tbs. vinegar |
| Pinch sugar and white pepper |
| ¼ cup pistachios |

Drop the pasta into boiling, salted water and cook for 6 minutes. Rinse and drain. Leave to cool. • Cut the ham into thin strips. Pit the olives and halve them. Crumble cheese into pieces. Trim, wash and cut the basil into thin strips. • In a bowl, mix together the vinegar, pinch of salt, sugar, pepper and oil. • Chop the pistachios. Mix the pasta with the cheese, ham, olives and basil. • Pour over the dressing. Toss well and leave for 30 minutes. • Sprinkle with the pistachios.

Variation: Instead of gorgonzola cheese use melon for a change or instead of basil use lemon.

Roman Pasta Salad

Lengthy preparation time

500 calories per serving
Preparation time: 1 hour

| 1¾ cups rigatoni |
| 4 qts. water |
| 1 tsp. salt |
| 2 carrots |
| 2 cups green beans |
| 2 cups green peas |
| 3 tomatoes |
| ¼ lb. Italian salami (thinly sliced) |
| 2 tbs. green and black olives |
| 6 anchovies |
| 2 tbs. capers |
| 3 tbs. vinegar |
| ¼ cup oil |
| Pinch salt, black pepper and sugar |
| 3 tbs. dried chives |

Put the pasta into boiling, salted water and cook until "al dente." • Peel, wash and cut the carrots into slices. • Wash, trim and cut the green beans into pieces. Boil in salted water for 12 minutes. • Boil the carrots and peas for 5 minutes. • Wash and dry the tomatoes. Cut into eighths. • Cut the salami into thin slices. • Pit the green and black olives and halve them. • Chop the anchovies and mix together with the capers, vinegar, oil and spices. • Drain the pasta and mix with the vegetables, tomatoes, salami, olives and dressing. Add the chives and leave covered for approximately 1 hour.

Amsterdam Pasta Salad

Economical, easy to prepare

480 calories per serving
Preparation time: 40 minutes

1¼ cups pasta (rigatoni or pasta twists)
2½ qts. water
1 tsp. salt
4 hard-boiled eggs
6 small tomatoes
1 small cucumber
1 red pepper
7 oz. corned beef
Pinch salt, freshly ground white pepper
Pinch sugar and garlic powder
2 tbs. vinegar
½ bunch parsley
3 tbs. oil

Drop pasta into boiling, salted water and cook until "al dente." Rinse and drain. • Peel eggs and cut into quarters. • Wash, dry and slice tomatoes and cucumber. • Halve the pepper, remove the core and seeds. Wash, dry and shred finely. • Slice the corned beef. • In a bowl, mix together the pasta, vegetables, corned beef and eggs. Add the dressing and toss well. • Cover and leave for 30 minutes at room temperature. • Wash and chop the parsley and sprinkle on top before serving.

Danish Pasta Salad

Economical, easy to prepare

740 calories per serving
Preparation time: 30 minutes
Cooling time: 1 hour

1 cup water
1 tsp. salt
1 tsp. oil
1¼ cup pasta (rigatoni or pasta bow ties)
1¼ cups frozen peas and carrots
Pinch salt, fresh ground black pepper
2 slices pineapple
1 large gherkin pickle
1¼ cups cooked ham without fat
1¾ cups mayonnaise
3 tbs. lemon juice
2 tbs. pineapple juice
3 tbs. milk
½ tsp. curry powder

Drop the pasta into boiling, salted water and cook until tender. • Rinse and drain well. • Boil the peas and carrots in 4 tbs. of water. Add salt and pepper and simmer for another 4 minutes. • Leave to cool. • Remove the rind from the pineapple and cut into small pieces. • Dice the ham and gherkin pickle. • In a bowl, mix together the mayonnaise, lemon and pineapple juice. Season with salt and pepper and curry powder to taste. • Pour over the pasta. Add vegetables, gherkin pickle, tomatoes, pineapple and ham and mix well together. • Cover and leave for 1 hour in a cool place. • Season to taste before serving.

Californian Pasta Salad with Chicken

Expensive

740 calories per serving
Preparation time: 45 minutes

½ roasted chicken
1 cup rigatoni
2 qts. water
1 tsp. salt
¾ cup gouda cheese
1 small endive
1 cup purple grapes
¾ cup full fat yogurt
1¼ cups cream
1 bunch mixed herbs (e.g. basil, chives, thyme)
Pinch salt, fresh ground white pepper and paprika powder
½ lemon

Skin and bone the chicken. Cut into small pieces. • Drop the pasta into boiling salted water and cook until tender. Rinse and drain. • Dice the cheese. Wash and drain the lettuce. Tear into pieces. Wash and de-seed the grapes. Cut into halves. • In a bowl, mix together the meat, pasta salad and grapes. • Mix the yogurt and cream. • Wash, dry and chop the herbs and pour over the yogurt mixture. Add spices and lemon juice and toss well. • Pour the dressing over the salad. Mix well. Cover and leave for 45 minutes.

Variation: Instead of grapes use pineapple or chopped walnuts.

Exotic Pasta Salads

Specialty, easy to prepare

640 calories per serving
Preparation time: 1 hour

2 qts. water	
1 tsp. salt	
6 tbs. oil	
1 cup tagliatelle	
4 chicken breasts	
1 tsp. coriander	
2 tsp. curry powder	
1 pinch white pepper	
4 tbs. marsala wine	
½ cup almonds	
2 bananas	
1 tbs. lemon juice	
2 tbs. raisins	
¼ cup light soy sauce	

Place the chicken breasts in a large bowl and coat with ½ tsp. coriander, curry powder, salt and pepper. • Heat the oil in a saucepan. Add the chicken and brown all sides. Pour over the Marsala wine and simmer on low heat for 5 minutes. Leave to cool reserving the stock. • Pour boiling water over the almonds. Peel and fry in a saucepan until golden brown. • Peel and slice the bananas and sprinkle with lemon juice. • Wash and dry the raisins. • Dice the chicken and cut into pieces. Cook tagliatelle for 8–10 minutes in boiling, salted water. Drain and refresh in cold water. • In a bowl, mix together the coriander, remaining curry powder, soy sauce, salt and oil. Add the chicken, stock, bananas, almonds and raisins and toss well. • Mix with the pasta. Leave in a cool place for 2 hours. Season to taste before serving.

Arabian Pasta Salad

Economical

500 calories per serving
Preparation time: 20 minutes

1¾ cups rigatoni	
4 qts. water	
1 tsp. salt	
1 cucumber	
1 jar pickled pumpkin	
½ cup Pecorino cheese	
½ bunch dill	
½ lemon	
1 tbs. apple juice	
1 cup full fat yogurt	
1 tbs. mayonnaise	
5 mint leaves	
2 tbs. sesame seeds.	

Put the pasta into boiling, salted water and cook until "al dente." • Peel and dice the cucumber. • Crumble the Pecorino cheese into pieces. • Wash, dry and chop the dill and mix together with the lemon juice, apple juice and chopped dill. • Wash, dry and chop the mint leaves. • In a bowl, mix together the pasta, cucumber, pumpkin, Pecorino cheese and mint. • Pour over lemon juice mixture, toss well and leave for 30 minutes. • Fry the sesame seeds in a saucepan until golden brown, stirring constantly. • Sprinkle on top of the salad before serving.

Pasta Salad with Tuna Fish

Expensive

450 calories per serving
Preparation time: 30 minutes

1¼ cups pasta bowties	
2½ qts. water	
1 tsp. salt	
1 can tuna fish in oil	
¼ lb. shrimp	
2 slices pineapple	
1 cooking apple	
2 tbs. lemon juice	
1 small onion	
1 tbs. walnut oil	
Pinch salt and freshly ground white pepper	
½ tsp. curry powder	
1 tbs. pineapple juice	
1 tbs. mustard	

Put the pasta into boiling, salted water and cook for 10 minutes until "al dente." Drain the tuna fish, reserving the oil. • Dice the pineapple slices. • Peel, core and quarter the apple. Cut into thin slices and sprinkle with lemon juice. • Peel and chop the onion. • Add the remaining lemon juice, salt, pepper, oil, curry powder, pineapple juice, mustard and the tuna fish oil. Mix well. • Stir in the pasta. Flake the tuna fish and add to the salad together with the shrimp, apple slices and pineapple pieces. Mix well.

Pasta and Smoked Trout Salad

Easy to prepare, expensive

450 calories per serving
Preparation time: 45 minutes

1¼ cups pasta spirals	
2½ qts. water	
1 tsp. salt	
4 smoked fillets of trout	
2¼ cups tomatoes	
2 gherkin pickles	
1 white onion	
3 tbs. vinegar	
½ tsp. salt	
Pinch white pepper and sugar	
3 tbs. olive oil	
1 bunch chives and chervil	

Put the pasta into boiling, salted water and cook for 8 minutes until "al dente." Cut the trout fillets into small portions. • Put tomatoes into boiling water for 10 seconds, then place immediately into a bowl of cold water. Drain and skin the tomatoes, remove the seeds and cut into eighths. • Dice the gherkin pickles. Peel and chop the onion. Add vinegar, salt, pepper, sugar and oil and stir into the cold pasta. Add the trout pieces, tomatoes and gherkin pickles. Mix well. • Season to taste before serving.

Tagliatelle with Red Lentils

Wholemeal recipe, easy to prepare

500 calories per serving
Preparation time: 45 minutes

¼ cup dried figs and apricots
2½ cups red lentils
2 cups water
½ bay leaf
2 tsp. vegetable broth
2 qts. water
1 tsp. salt
1 cup wholewheat tagliatelle
2 oz. smoked ham
¼ cup dates
1¾ cups sour cream
3 tbs. lemon juice
Pinch freshly ground white pepper
1 tbs. chopped parsley

Wash the figs and apricots; put in a bowl and pour over with boiling water. Cover and leave for approximately 15 minutes. • Drop the lentils into boiling water. Add the bay leaf and vegetable broth and simmer on a low heat for 10 minutes. • Put the pasta into boiling, salted water and cook for approximately 10 minutes until "al dente." Drain and rinse the pasta and lentils under cold running water. • Cut the smoked ham into thin strips. • Drain the figs and apricots and cut into thin strips. Pit the dates and cut into pieces. • In a bowl, mix together the sour cream, 2 tbs. lemon juice and pepper. Add all the chopped and cooked ingredients and mix well. Add lemon juice and pepper to taste. • Leave at room temperature for 15 minutes before serving.

Spaghetti Salad with Chicken

Economical, easy to prepare

550 calories per serving
Preparation time: 40 minutes

2½ qts. water	
1 tsp. salt	
1¼ cups spaghetti	
3 carrots	
½ roast chicken	
1 cup Chinese cabbage	
1 celery	
1 cup cucumber	
3 tbs. vinegar	
½ tsp. salt	
Pinch sugar	
Pinch white pepper	
½ tsp. soy sauce	
3 tbs. sesame oil	
2 tbs. dried chives	

Break the spaghetti in pieces. Drop into boiling, salted water and cook for 8 minutes until cooked "al dente." • Peel the carrots and cut into thin strips. Blanch for 2 minutes. Drain and leave to cool. • Skin and bone the chicken. Cut into 1 in. pieces. • Cut the Chinese cabbage into thin strips. Rinse under cold running water and drain. • Wash and finely shred the celery. • Peel, wash, halve and seed the cucumber. Cut into small pieces. • Mix together the vinegar, salt, sugar, pepper and soy sauce. Fold into the oil. • Add the spaghetti, chicken and vegetables. • Sprinkle with chives.

Chickpea and Pasta Salad

Lengthy preparation time

640 calories per serving
Soaking time: 12 hours
Preparation time: 30 minutes

1 cup chickpeas	
2 tsp. vegetable broth	
½ bay leaf	
1¼ cups peeled almonds	
1 cup pasta twists	
2 qts. water	
1 tsp. salt	
2 cans mandarin orange segments	
1¾ cups cottage cheese	
1 cup cream	
2 pinches salt and curry powder	
2 tbs. lemon juice	

Soak the chickpeas overnight in 4 cups of cold water. • Next day, place the chickpeas together with the vegetable broth and the bay leaf into a large saucepan and simmer for 40 minutes. Drain. • Roast the almonds in a dry pan. • Drop the pasta into boiling salted water and cook for 8 minutes. Rinse and drain. • Cut the almonds into thin pieces. • Drain the mandarins. • In a bowl mix together the cottage cheese, cream, salt, curry powder and lemon juice. • Pour in all the remaining ingredients and mix well. • Add the lemon juice to taste.

Wholewheat Pasta Salad with Chicken

Wholemeal Recipe

520 calories per serving
Preparation time: 50 minutes

| 1 cup chickpeas |
| 2 tsp. vegetable broth |
| 1 cup wholewheat pasta (pasta twists or rigatoni) |
| 2 qts. water |
| 1 tsp. salt |
| 1 roasted chicken |
| 2 ripe avocados |
| ½ cup mushrooms |
| ½ cup carrots |
| 1¼ cups cream |
| 1 tsp. honey and salt |
| 3 tbs. lemon juice |
| Pinch freshly ground white pepper |
| 2 tbs. chopped parsley |

Soak the chickpeas overnight in 4 cups of cold water. • The next day, place the chickpeas in a large saucepan together with the vegetable broth and simmer on low heat for 40 minutes. • Drop the pasta into boiling, salted water and cook for 8–10 minutes. Drain and rinse. • Skin and bone the chicken and cut the meat into pieces. Halve and pit the avocados and cut them into pieces. • Clean the mushrooms, remove the stalks and slice finely. • Peel and coarsely grate the carrots. • In a bowl mix together the cream, honey, salt, 2 tbs. lemon juice, pepper and parsley. • Stir in all the vegetables and meat. Mix well. • Leave the salad to stand for 15 minutes before serving. • Add lemon juice, salt and pepper to taste.

Pasta Salad with Peppers and Sweetcorn

Economical, easy to prepare

450 calories per serving
Preparation time: 1 hour

| 5 qts. water |
| 2 tsp. salt |
| 2¼ cups rigatoni |
| 2¼ cups frozen peas |
| 1 red pepper |
| 7 oz. cooked ham |
| 2¼ cups sweetcorn |
| 1 bunch mixed herbs (e.g. parsley, chives, basil and thyme) |
| 4 tsp. vinegar |
| 1 tsp. salt |
| ½ tsp. paprika powder and white pepper |
| Pinch garlic powder |
| 5 tbs. oil |
| 1 bunch radish |
| 2 hard boiled eggs |

Drop the pasta into boiling salted water until tender, yet firm to the bite. Drain and leave to cool. Wash, seed and dice the pepper. Drain the sweetcorn. Chop the herbs. Reserve 1 tbs. of mixed herbs. • Mix together the herbs, vinegar, salt, pepper, red pepper, garlic powder and oil. • Slice the radishes. Peel the eggs and cut into eighths. • In a bowl mix together the pasta, peas, diced red pepper, ham, sweetcorn and half of the radishes. Add the marinade. • Place the eggs and radish slices on top. Sprinkle with the remaining herbs.

Wholewheat Pasta and Pea Salad

Wholemeal Recipe

450 calories per serving
Preparation time: 45 minutes

1 cup wholewheat pasta twists
2 qts. water
1 tsp. salt
1 green pepper
2 onions
1¼ cups green peas
1 can tuna fish
1 cup shredded Pecorino cheese
3 tbs. sesame oil and tarragon vinegar
2 tbs. freshly chopped basil and thyme
2 tbs. dried chives
Pinch black pepper
1 tsp. paprika powder
1 large tomato

Drop the pasta into boiling salted water and cook for 8–10 minutes. • Wash the green pepper. Remove seeds and membranes, then slice. • Peel, halve and slice the onions. • Drain the pasta. Reserve the water. Bring to a boil. Drop in the green pepper and onions and blanch for 2 minutes. • Drop the peas into ¼ cup of boiling water and cook for 5 minutes. • Flake the tuna fish. • Place the tuna fish liquid in a bowl. Add the shredded cheese, oil, vinegar, herbs, pepper and paprika powder. Mix well. Add onions and peas, slice the tomatoes and mix into the salad. • Leave the salad for 5 minutes before serving.

Wholewheat Pasta and Dandelion Salad

Wholemeal Recipe

560 calories per serving
Preparation time: 1 hour

1 cup red soybeans
4 cups water
1 bay leaf
5 oz. lean bacon
¼ cup sunflower oil
2 qts. water
1 tsp. salt
1 cup wholewheat pasta
¼ cup dandelion
¼ cup vinegar
½ tsp. salt
¼ tsp. freshly ground black pepper.

Soak the beans in plenty of cold water for about 12 hours. • The next day, bring the beans to a boil. Add the bay leaf and cook for 35–40 minutes until tender. Drain well. Dice the bacon and fry in a saucepan until crispy. • Drop the pasta into boiling, salted water and cook for 10 minutes, until "al dente." Rinse and drain well. • Wash and finely chop the dandelion leaves. • In a bowl, mix together the noodles, dandelion leaves, bacon, vinegar, salt and pepper. • Leave to cool. • Add vinegar, salt and pepper to taste before serving.

Pasta and Broccoli Salad

Wholemeal recipe, easy to prepare

380 calories per serving
Preparation time: 45 minutes

2 qts. water
1 tsp. salt
1¼ cups broccoli
¾ cup millet spaghetti
1 zucchini
2 tomatoes
2 hard boiled eggs
¼ cup walnuts
1 cup cream
2 tbs. salt
Pinch mixed spices
Pinch freshly ground white pepper
1 tbs. dried chives

Trim and rinse the broccoli, discarding any woody stems. Cut into 1¼ in. pieces. • Drop the pasta and broccoli into boiling, salted water and cook for 10 minutes until "al dente." • Trim and wash the zucchini and tomatoes and cut into pieces. • Peel the eggs and chop finely. Chop the walnuts. • In a bowl, mix together pasta, vegetables, tomatoes, eggs and nuts. Add the cream, lemon juice, salt and pinch of mixed spices and pepper. Add the chives. • Leave the salad for 5 minutes before serving. Add the lemon juice, salt and pepper to taste.

Hot Pasta Salads

Quick and easy to prepare

500 calories per serving
Preparation time: 30 minutes

1¼ cups capellini (e.g. very thin spaghetti)
2½ qts. water
1 tsp. salt
1 tsp. oil
1¼ cups broccoli
4 cups water
1 tsp. salt
2 tbs. lemon juice
Pinch freshly ground nutmeg
¾ cup Pecorino cheese
6 tbs. olive oil
1 clove garlic
¼ cup vinegar

Drop the spaghetti into boiling, salted water and cook for 6–8 minutes until tender. Rinse and drain. • Trim and rinse the broccoli, discarding any woody stems. Cut into small pieces. • Drop the broccoli into boiling, salted water and blanch for 2 minutes. Drain and sprinkle with nutmeg. • Dice the Pecorino. • Peel and finely chop the garlic and fry in a saucepan for half a minute. Add the vinegar and oil. • In a bowl, mix together all the ingredients. Serve warm.

Pasta and Bacon Salad

Quick and easy to prepare

570 calories per serving
Preparation time: 25 minutes

2½ qts. water
1 tsp. salt
1¼ cups wholewheat pasta (pasta twists or rigatoni)
1 small endive
1 onion
1 bunch chives
1 tsp. oil
7 oz. lean bacon (thin sliced)
2–4 tbs. vinegar
Pinch cayenne pepper

Drop the pasta into boiling salted water and cook for 8–10 minutes until "al dente." Rinse and drain. • Clean, wash and dry the endive and cut into thin strips. Peel and dice the onion. Wash and chop the chives. • Fry the bacon in a saucepan until crispy and dry on paper towel. • Fry the onion in a saucepan until transparent. Take away from heat. Add the vinegar and cayenne pepper. • In a bowl, mix together the pasta, endive, chives and the warm marinade. • Sprinkle the crispy bacon on top. Serve immediately.

Pasta Salad with Cream and Herbs

Lengthy cooking time

550 calories per serving
Preparation time: 1 hour

1 cup gnocchi
2 qts. water
1 tsp. salt
½ cup oil
2¼ cups red peppers
7 oz. tuna fish
2 small onions
5 hard boiled eggs
2 tbs. dill, chervil, parsley, cardamon
1 clove garlic
1 tbs. mustard
¼ cup lowfat yogurt
Pinch salt and freshly ground white pepper
½ cup green olives without pits

Drop the pasta into boiling, salted water and cook for approximately 8 minutes until tender. Rinse and drain. • Wash the red peppers, remove seeds and membranes, then cut into slices. • Drain and flake the tuna fish. Peel the onions and cut into rings. Halve the eggs. • Take out the egg yolks and mix together with the oil. • Wash, dry and chop the herbs. • In a bowl mix together the herbs, mustard, yogurt, egg yolks and finely chopped garlic. Add salt and pepper to taste. • Mix this together with the sauce, pasta, peppers, onion rings, tuna fish and olives. • Leave for 2 hours in a cool place.

Tagliatelle Verde Salad

Lengthy cooking time

450 calories per serving
Preparation time: 1 hour

1 cup tagliatelle verde
8 cups water
1 tsp. salt
1 tsp. oil
1¼ cups zucchini
2¼ cups asparagus
8 tbs. olive oil
Pinch of salt and freshly ground black pepper
3 oz. lean bacon
3 scallions
1 clove garlic
4 tbs. vinegar
1 tbs. capers
3 tbs. chopped parsley
1 tbs. chopped basil
Pinch sugar

1 tbs. grated Parmesan cheese

Drop the pasta into boiling, salted water and cook until "al dente." Rinse and drain. • Top and tail the zucchini, rinse and dry. Slice thinly in diagonal slices. • Wash the asparagus. Remove woody parts and scales, then cut into ¾ in. lengths. • Fry the zucchini in 2 tbs. oil for 5 minutes. Add pinch of salt and pepper. • Leave to cool. • Drop the asparagus into salted water and cook for 10–15 minutes. Drain well. • Dice the bacon and fry in 1 tbs. oil. Cut the onions into rings. • Peel and crush the garlic and mix together with vinegar, remaining salt, pepper, capers, parsley, basil, sugar and Parmesan cheese. Add the remaining oil, vegetables, pasta and bacon. • Leave for one hour before serving.

Pasta Salad with Spring Vegetables

Economical, easy to prepare

520 calories per serving
Preparation time: 45 minutes

4 qts. water
2 tsp. salt
1¾ cups pasta twists
1 small cucumber
1 green pepper
4 tomatoes
1 kohlrabi
9 oz. beef sausage (cooked)
4 tbs. vinegar
½ tsp. salt
Pinch white pepper and curry powder
1 small onion
1 clove garlic
4 tbs. oil
½ bunch chives and parsley
1 bunch watercress

Drop the pasta into boiling, salted water and cook until "al dente." Rinse and drain. • Peel and slice the cucumber. • Wash the peppers. Remove seeds and membranes then slice. • Wash and dry tomatoes, then cut into eighths. • Trim, wash and peel kohlrabi and cut into thin strips. Skin and dice the sausage. • Mix together the vinegar, salt, pepper and curry. • Peel the onion and grate into the marinade. • Peel and crush the garlic and add to the marinade. Add the oil. • Mix all the remaining ingredients together and fold into the marinade. • Toss well. • Sprinkle the chopped herbs on top. • Use the watercress as garnish.

Pasta Salad with Green Beans

Economical, quick

480 calories per serving
Preparation time: 40 minutes

3 qts. water
1 tsp. salt
1¼ cups pasta quills
1¼ cups string beans
¼ lb. beef sausage (cooked)
10 green stuffed olives
1 bunch parsley
1 onion
2 tbs. mayonnaise
1 cup sour cream
2 tbs. vinegar
Pinch salt and freshly ground black pepper

Drop the pasta into boiling, salted water and cook for 8–19 minutes until tender. • Top and tail the beans. Leave small beans whole, cut into 1½ in. pieces. Boil in salted water for 15 minutes. Drain well. Leave to cool. Reserve 3 tbs. of the cooking liquid. • Slice the sausages and the onions finely. • Wash and dry the parsley. Chop finely. Reserve one stem for the garnish. • Peel and chop the onion finely. Mix together with the mayonnaise, sour cream, vinegar, remaining cooking liquid and chopped parsley. • Mix together the pasta, beans, sausage, and the olives. Add to the marinade. Toss well. Season with salt and pepper to taste.

Vegetarian Pasta Salad

Economical, easy to prepare

620 calories per serving
Preparation time: 40 minutes

3 qts. water
1 tsp. salt
1¼ cups tagliatelle verde
2 green peppers
2 shallots
½ bunch parsley
1 bunch chives
¾ cup gorgonzola
3 tbs. vinegar
1¼ cup cream
Pinch of salt and freshly ground black pepper
1 hard boiled egg

Drop the noodles into boiling, salted water and cook for 8 minutes until "al dente." • Halve the peppers, remove the seeds and core, wash and dry. Cut into strips. • Peel and chop the shallots. • Wash, dry and chop the parsley and chives. • Crush the gorgonzola and mix together with vinegar, cream, salt, pepper, shallots and herbs. • Reserve 1 tbs. of chives for the garnish. • Peel and chop the egg. • Mix together the pasta and green peppers. Add the cheese sauce. • Garnish with egg and chives before serving.

Pasta Salad with Shrimp

Expensive, quick to prepare

570 calories per serving
Preparation time: 40 minutes

10 cups water	
1 tsp. salt	
1¼ cup rigatoni	
7 oz. shrimp	
2 tbs. lemon juice	
1 honeydew melon	
1 avocado	
1 cup celery	
1 bunch dill	
2 tbs. mayonnaise	
1¼ cups full fat yogurt	
3 tbs. cream	
2 tbs. cognac	
Pinch salt, white pepper and cayenne pepper	

Drop the pasta into boiling, salted water and cook for 8 minutes until "al dente." • Rinse and drain the shrimp. Sprinkle with 2 tbs. lemon juice. • Peel and seed the melon and cut into cubes. • Cut the avocado into halves. Take out the pit and cut into slices. Sprinkle with the remaining lemon juice. • Scrub the celery, string it, cut into slices. • Wash, dry and chop the dill. • Mix together the mayonnaise with the remaining ingredients. Add the dill, pasta, shrimp, melon, avocado and celery. Toss well. • Garnish with dill before serving.

Pasta Salad with Oranges

Economical, easy to prepare

430 calories per serving
Preparation time: 40 minutes

10 cups water	
1 tsp. salt	
1¼ cup pasta bowties	
1 cucumber	
2 onions	
2 oranges	
1 red apple	
3 tbs. lemon juice	
1¼ cups full fat yogurt	
1 cup sour cream	
1 tbs. mayonnaise	
3 tbs. orange juice	
Pinch salt, sugar and freshly ground white pepper	

Drop the pasta into boiling, salted water and cook for 8 minutes until "al dente." Peel and slice the cucumber. Peel and cut the onions into thin rings. • Peel the oranges, cut into segments, discarding pits and membrane. • Peel, dry, core and slice the apple. Sprinkle with lemon juice. • In a bowl, mix together the yogurt, cream, mayonnaise, orange juice, salt, sugar and pepper. • Add the pasta, cucumber, onions, oranges and apples. Toss well.

Pasta Salad with Mussels

Expensive

430 calories per serving
Preparation time: 1 hour

4½ lbs. mussels
2 cloves garlic
1 large tomato
1 bunch basil or 1 tsp. dried basil
8 tbs. olive oil
6 peppercorns
Pinch sugar
½ cup white wine
1¼ cups pasta shells
10 cups water
1 tsp. salt
1 green pepper
1 bunch parsley
4 tbs. vinegar
Pinch of salt and cayenne pepper

Brush the mussels clean under cold running water. Do not use mussels with open shells. • Peel and chop the garlic. Wash and dice the tomatoes. Chop the basil leaves. • Fry the garlic with 2 tbs. oil in a saucepan. Add the tomato, half of the basil, peppercorns, sugar and wine. • Add the water and mussels and blanch for 5 minutes on high heat. • Unopened shells must be thrown away. Reserve the cooking liquid. • Take out the mussel meat and boil in 3 tbs. of cooking liquid. • Drop the pasta into boiling, salted water and cook for 8 minutes until "al dente." Rinse and drain. • Chop the green pepper. • Mix the cooking liquid from the mussels, vinegar and oil together and add all the herbs. Season with salt and cayenne pepper. Add the pasta, peppers and mussels.

Chinese White Noodle Salad with Crabmeat

Specialty from China, expensive

500 calories per serving
Preparation time: 1 hour

| 8 cups water |
| 1 cup Chinese white noodles |
| 8 black Chinese dried mushrooms (Mu Err) |
| 14 oz. crabmeat |
| 4 scallions |
| 1 small can water chestnuts |
| 1 small can bamboo shoots |
| 1 tsp. salt |
| 2 tbs. soy sauce and sweet and sour sauce |
| Few drops hot chili sauce |
| 8 tbs. oil |
| 3 tbs. lemon juice |

Place ¾ cup of pasta and same of the mushrooms into two separate bowls. • Pour over boiling water and soak for 30 minutes. • Divide the crabmeat into small pieces. • Wash, dry and slice the scallions into strips. • Rinse, drain and slice the chestnuts and bamboo shoots into thin strips. • Drain the mushrooms and cut into strips. • Drain the pasta and place in a bowl together with the chopped ingredients, salt, soy sauce, sweet and sour sauce, chili sauce and 3 tbs. oil. Mix well together. • Heat the remaining oil in a saucepan and fry the remaining pasta until soft. • Dry on paper towel and sprinkle over the salad. • Pour the lemon juice on top.

Noodle Salad with Cooked Beef

Easy and quick to prepare

360 calories per serving
Preparation time: 30 minutes

| 3 qts. water |
| 1½ tsp. salt |
| 2¼ cups Chinese egg noodles |
| 2 cups soybeans |
| ½ lb. cooked beef |
| 2 bunches radishes |
| 4 scallions |
| 5 tbs. oil |
| ½ tsp. salt |
| 3 tbs. vinegar |
| Pinch white pepper |
| 2 tbs. soy sauce |
| 1 tbs. sugar |

Drop the noodles into boiling, salted water and cook for 6–8 minutes until tender. Rinse and drain. • Place the soybeans in boiling water for just a few seconds. • Drain and rinse under cold running water. • Cut the beef into ¼ in. cubes. Clean, wash and slice the radishes. Wash scallions under lukewarm water and slice into thin strips. • Mix the noodles with oil. • Divide the noodles into four portions and place into four serving dishes. • Mix the oil with the beef and soybeans and add to the noodles. • Sprinkle the radishes and scallions on top.

Index